PANTS FOR ANY BODY
by Pati Palmer and Susan Pletsch

Revised Expanded Edition

Design and Technical Illustration by
Linda Wisner

Fashion Illustrations by
Patty Andersen

Cover Art by
Priscilla F. Lee

Whenever brand names are mentioned, it is only to indicate to the consumer products which we have personally tested and with which we have been pleased. It is also meant to save our students time. There may be other products that are comparable to aid you in your sewing.

Library of Congress Catalog Card No. 82-61290

Published by Palmer/Pletsch Associates, P.O. Box 12046,
Portland, Oregon 97212-0046

Design and production by Brown/Wisner, Eugene, Oregon.
Technical illustrations by Linda Wisner, Alison McKinley,
Kathy Howell and Debralynn Berrow.
Printed by The Irwin Hodson Company, Portland, Oregon, U.S.A.

ISBN 0-935278-08-7

Table of Contents

Pati Palmer   Susan Pletsch

About the authors . . .

Pati Palmer and Susan Pletsch have co-authored four sewing books, established their own publishing company, and now travel across North America teaching fashion sewing seminars. Their most recent accomplishments include designing patterns for the McCall Pattern Company and coordinating a line of elegant fabrics.

Pati and Susan met while educational representatives for the Armo Company, a shaping fabrics manufacturer. Pati has also been Corporate Home Economist for an Oregon department store, as well as buyer of sewing notions. She graduated from Oregon State University with a B.S. in Home Economics, and is active in the American Home Economics Association, Home Economists in Business, and Fashion Group.

Susan has been a home economist with Talon Consumer Education, where she traveled extensively giving consumer and educator workshops. She was also a free-lance home economist with many sewing related firms. Susan graduated from Arizona State University and taught home economics to special education students. She is affiliated with the American Home Economics Association and Home Economists in Business.

Pati and Susan are individually recognized for their sewing skills and teaching and lecturing abilities. Together they produce an unbeatable combination of knowledge, personality and talent.

Our first edition of **Pants for Any Body** emphasized measuring as a way to achieve perfect fit. Then we found that the only measurements people could accurately take on themselves were length and width — crotch measurements were virtually impossible. Since then in our nationwide seminars we've fitted over 50,000 people in pants made from a commercial pattern in ¼" gingham checked fabric. Gingham takes away all the guesswork! So, in our revised **Pants for Any Body**, we strongly emphasize this easier, more accurate gingham method and practically **no** measuring!

Our pant fitting philosophy is different than most:

1. **We use commercial patterns** rather than teaching you to draft your own. After all, patterns are one of the least expensive ingredients in sewing pants, and the most time consuming to create yourself. All the major pattern companies use a "sloper" or master pattern to develop their designs and all are similar in shape. We'll teach you how to find out where your body varies from commercial patterns and how to make alterations to compensate for those differences. You will then have to make those alterations on ANY PATTERN YOU SEW. Your full tummy doesn't go away just because you switched from a Butterick to a McCall's pattern!

2. **We don't promise you a perfect pattern** that you can cut, sew, and wear without ever trying on. That's impossible unless you **never** fluctuate one ounce in weight, **never** make a cutting error (⅛" error times 8 seam allowances around a pant can make each pair 1" different in size), and **always** use exactly the same fabric (every fabric fits differently). You can, however, alter a pattern to be close to your size and shape and then use our Fit-As-You-Sew™ system to create **PERFECT PANTS.**

3. **You can use ANY fabric with ANY pattern.** You don't need a special pattern for knits and another for woven fabrics. Using our same Fit-As-You-Sew™ system, you can get good fit with any fabric.

4. **A great looking pant goes beyond good fit!** It is also selecting the best style for your figure, the best fabric for that style, and sewing beautiful pant details. Pockets that gap, zippers that pucker, and pleats that pooch all detract from good fit. We think choosing the right pattern, fabric, and sewing techniques together form the "great pants package deal". We'll even share some of our favorite tips for FAST pant sewing — how about "Great Pants in 3 Hours"!!

After fitting 50,000 bodies, we know we can fit pants to ANY body — even yours!

What style pant is best for your figure? Our philosophy is that any figure type can wear any style as long as it fits properly. Even a person with a large tummy can look nice in a pant with a waistband and a tucked-in blouse. Good fit can make you look 10 pounds thinner! With pants that fit, you will be liberated to wear more variety and to look more fashionable!

What is Good Fit?

Good fit means pants are comfortable and wrinkle free

Good fit means pants hang straight

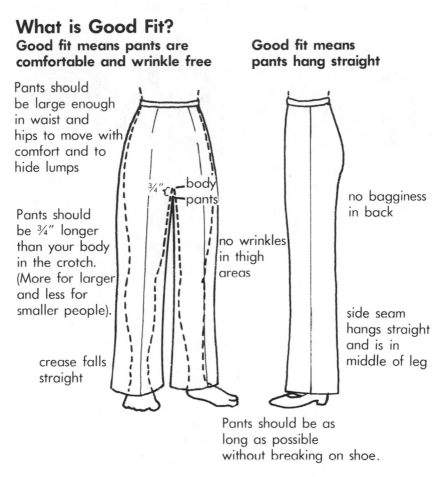

Pants should be large enough in waist and hips to move with comfort and to hide lumps

¾" — body — pants

Pants should be ¾" longer than your body in the crotch. (More for larger and less for smaller people).

no wrinkles in thigh areas

no bagginess in back

side seam hangs straight and is in middle of leg

crease falls straight

Pants should be as long as possible without breaking on shoe.

Which Pant Styles are Most Flattering

Tight pants show off your shape! So unless your shape is perfect, looser pants are universally better for both thinner and heavier bodies.

The most flattering pants of all are trousers. They are fuller so they don't reveal lumps and bumps and have lots of vertical lines to make you look taller and slimmer. Even your tummy will look smaller in trousers, if they fit properly.

True trousers have slanted pockets, fly front and tucks — lots of vertical lines.

Modified trousers have either tucks, slanted pockets, or perhaps just a fly front zipper. They have fewer vertical lines than trousers, so are less slimming.

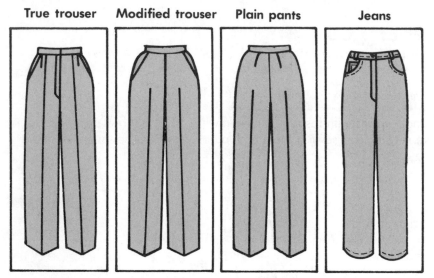

| True trouser | Modified trouser | Plain pants | Jeans |

Plain pants have little camouflage value and are best on figures with nothing to hide.

Traditional jeans — tight everywhere — had a functional beginning. We didn't need extra crotch length or thigh room when riding on horseback. In fact, the extra room would cause chafing and saddle sores! The function has changed, but the fit is the same — tight!

Pattern Envelope Tells All

Pattern envelopes use line drawings to show true pant shape (straight versus flared legs, type of waistline, number of darts, etc.). They also state the bottom width and the pant length. Once you find **your** most flattering length and leg width, you can compare them with other styles in the pattern books.

Width at lower edge (each leg)					
Pants A, B	20	20½	21	21½	22
Finished side length from waist					
Pants A, B	40½	40¾	41	41¼	41½

Attractive Waistband Widths

The average waistband width used by pattern companies is 1¼". If you are short waisted, try a narrower band (½-1"), a contour band (pg. 92), facing the waistline (pg. 56) or wear tunics, cardigans, long vests, or blazers with your pants to elongate your waist. If you are long waisted, try wide waistbands (1½-2") and interesting wide belts. If your waist fluctuates in size daily, try our elastic back band (pg. 54) or convert any style to our separate elastic casing that looks like a fashionable waistband (pg. 53). If waistbands always wrinkle, use Armo-flexxx or Ban-Rol, truly non-roll interfacings (pg. 87).

Fashion Dictates Pant Length

Length varies with fashion, but even when fashion shows shorter pants, we recommend sewing them as long as possible. The longer the pant leg, the longer your legs will appear.

Here's how fashion dictates length:

 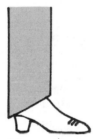  

| Narrow legs must be shorter in length. | Narrow legs can be made longer in back. | Straight legs can touch top of shoe in front. | Wide legs can go to the floor. |

Length also varies with the height of heel you wear. When establishing length, try pants on with the shoes you plan to wear with them.

Cuffs or No Cuffs

Cuffs shorten your legs because they are a horizontal line.

Flattering Fabrics

If you are heavy and/or short, avoid bulky fabrics, tweeds, plaids, and stiff fabrics. They add visual weight. If you are tall and thin, you may love these. Wool gabardine, polyester gabardine, and linen are universally flattering pant fabrics. They are heavy enough to drape over and camouflage body bulges, yet not so heavy or textured that they add bulk.

Wearable Pant Colors

The most versatile colors are the basics, such as taupe, beige, black, brown, ecru, grey and navy; because you can wear so many different colored tops with these, including neutrals. If you make peach pants, you will be limiting your choices. If you are on a budget, a year-round fabric and color are best. Susan has built a wardrobe around a pair of black wool gabardine pants. She wears them all year (since wool breaths and insulates) and for daytime and evening. Pati built a wardrobe around a 3-piece navy polyester gabardine suit when she first began her career. It took her everywhere, in every season, and was less expensive than the wool gabardine.

Use Color to Your Advantage

Your eye sees light, bright and shiny colors first, so if you want to de-emphasize your hip width, avoid these colors on the bottom. Use them to call attention to your face. Study these drawings to see how color can enhance your figure:

Very light top and dark bottom with strong contrast shortens figure with horizontal line.

Medium light top and medium dark bottom, doesn't cut the figure, but still draws eye to face.

Monochromatic (same color) top and bottom is elongating. Colors can be of slightly different shades.

Jacket and pant in same color create a full length vertical line. Light blouse draws eye to face. This is the most slimming look of all.

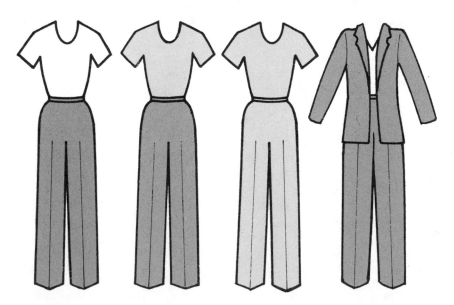

Building a Pant Wardrobe

Carry swatches of your wardrobe fabrics on a card in your purse to use for color matching while shopping. You will plan better and will look smarter on a much smaller budget.

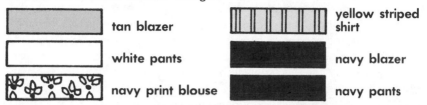

tan blazer	yellow striped shirt
white pants	navy blazer
navy print blouse	navy pants

When you buy fabric for pants, decide if it would be a good fabric for a jacket, then buy it all at one time as dye lots vary. There are so many different blacks, whites, and navies that you may **never** match the pants. We go one step further. We buy enough for pants, skirt and jacket at one time. The cutting advantage gained will often leave enough fabric for a free vest to be added when vests are in fashion.

Attractive Jacket Lengths

If the pants fit well, jacket length is not as crucial. As a general rule, jackets should be long enough to hide the derriere because if a jacket stops at the fullest part of the hip, it will emphasize hip width. Overall proportion must also be considered — a short person may look better in a shorter jacket. Before making a jacket, pin pattern pieces together and try on with the finished pants. A full length mirror will give you your answers.

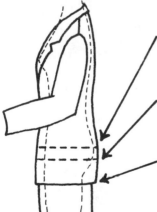

Above fullest part of hip — OK for thin hips and short people.

Just below fullest part of hip — a "compromise length" when fashion decrees "short jackets". If jacket is to be worn with **both** pants and skirts, this is best length.

Well below fullest part of hip — hides hips best and is safest length for average to tall people.

If the proportion doesn't seem right, try one of the following:

* Change shoes (shape and heel height)
* Change jacket length
* Pin pant legs narrower (see pg. 59)
* Match jacket and pant colors

Pant Shoes and Stockings

The wrong shoe can throw off the whole proportion of your outfit. Stockings are important too. If you want your legs to look their longest, ALWAYS blend your stockings and shoes with your pant color. If you wear a grey pant, a suntan stocking and a black shoe, all you will see is leg and it will look very spotty. For a tall, fashionable look with grey pants, we would suggest a grey or taupe shoe (the most versatile and seasonless shoe color!) and grey or sheer black stocking. A closed toe pump with a 2½" heel is a universally safe year-round shoe that can be worn with both pants and skirts. Out of date shoes and stockings can date you. Flip through fashion magazines looking at nothing but shoes and stockings for a quick fashion education.

Underwear for Pants

Practice looking in the mirror to see if your underwear shows before going out in public. Choose underwear that blends with your skin tone and look for soft elastic to minimize the "bikini bump" effect.

Watch Out For "The Tacky Look!"

Panty lines — look in the mirror before you go out. Any lines? Try pantyhose with built-in panties or to-the-waist-panties instead of bikinis.

Blouse lines — Pati simply pinks the lower edges of shirts so they are flat under pants. Also try tucking blouses into panties or pantyhose. You will be less likely to have panty or blouse lines with looser pants, firmer fabrics and lined or underlined pants.

1. Buy the right size pattern.

2. Cut to fit — the "easy way out" or the "it takes a little longer, but sure is worth it" way.

3. Fit-as-you-sew.

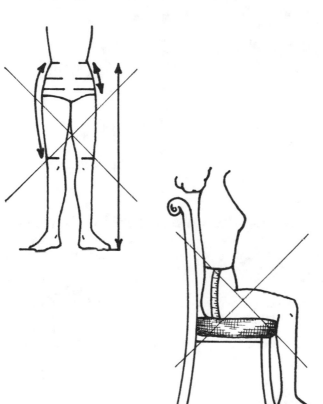

Take only two measurements from now on! Just your hip and waist measurements are all that's needed to buy the right size pattern. No more measuring every inch of your body. No more sitting on a chair to take crotch measurements. Why? Because it doesn't work for most people anyway!

We think our easy alternatives will revolutionize pant fitting!

Two Ways You Can Make Pants Fit

1. The "easy way out" method for lazy people with minor fitting problems (like Susan). This group basically fits into patterns (even ready-to-wear) with minor alterations, and really needs no more than "Pant Insurance".

- Buy pattern by hip size.

- Add "Pant Insurance" — cut "in-case" seam allowances (larger than normal "in-case" you need them) in common problem areas onto any pant.

- Fine tune the fit with our **Fit-As-You-Sew**™ System (pg. 41).

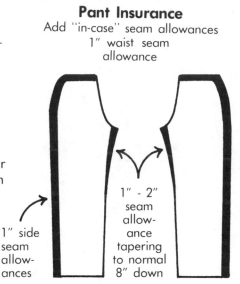

Pant Insurance
Add "in-case" seam allowances
1" waist seam
allowance

1" side seam allowances

1" - 2" seam allowance tapering to normal 8" down

2. The "it takes a little longer but sure is worth it" way for people who have never been able to fit into a pattern or to buy ready-made pants, because of just too many fitting problems.

- Select a basic style pattern.

- Add "in-case" seam allowances and crotch depth outlets (pg. 23).

- Sew the basic in ¼" gingham checked fabric.

- Fit gingham pant — See "You Can Fit Your Self — Fitting Problems and Solutions."

- Make same adjustments on basic pattern.

- Test altered pattern in any fabric using our **Fit-As-You-Sew**™ system (pg. 41).

4 Buy the Right Size Pattern

Ease is Built Into All Patterns

The difference between the size of your pants and your body is called "ease". Pattern companies automatically add ease to body measurements. The minimum amount allowed for "wiggle room" is called **comfort ease**. However, when designers want a style to fit looser or tighter, they add or subtract from standard comfort ease and call it **design ease** (pg. 17).

Comfort Ease

Width — All pattern companies allow a standard comfort ease of 1" in the waist and 2" in the hips.

Crotch Depth — Pattern companies allow a standard comfort ease of ¾" in the crotch depth. This means pants will hang down ¾" from the body.

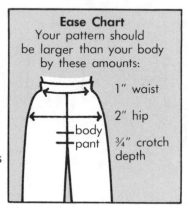

Ease Chart
Your pattern should be larger than your body by these amounts:

1" waist

2" hip

¾" crotch depth

Ease is Personal Preference

The amount of ease that **you** find comfortable varies with your size and the way you like your clothes to fit. To find out the amount of ease you prefer, try on various pants in your wardrobe and use our PINCH AND PULL TEST!

1. Pinch all the ease to one side. If you can pinch 1", that is 2" of ease since you are pinching double thickness.
Comfortable? If so, make all pants at least 2" larger than your body.

2. If you can pinch ½" that is 1" ease. Are pants comfortable? If not, cut pants larger.

3. If you can't pinch anything . . . Help! Hopefully they are jeans or a knit pant!

4. Now pull. Lift pants up and down to feel how far they hang down from your crotch. Do the pants that are comfortable seem to hang down ½", ¾", or 1"? This will tell you the amount of crotch depth ease you like.

Design Ease

Designers may use more or less ease than standard comfort ease in order to create a fashion look. Note the amount of ease and how it varies in waist, hip, and crotch depth in these styles:

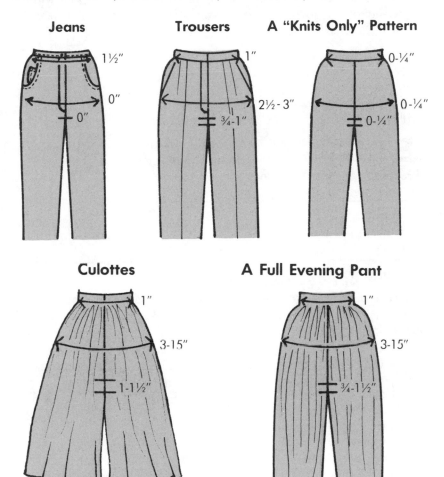

Jeans

1½"

0"

0"

Trousers

1"

2½-3"

¾-1"

A "Knits Only" Pattern

0-¼"

0-¼"

0-¼"

Culottes

1"

3-15"

1-1½"

A Full Evening Pant

1"

3-15"

¾-1½"

Measure the Pattern to Check Ease

The quickest way to find out how much larger a pattern is than your body (ease) is to measure the pattern in the same places. The best way to check crotch depth ease is to lay it on top of your basic pattern. If you don't have a basic, use "pant insurance" instead (pg. 14).

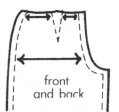

front and back

Buy Pant Patterns by Hip Measurement

When you buy by hip measurement, you will know the pant will be large enough to go around you even though you may still need to adjust the crotch or waist.

Stand in front of a full length mirror (to make sure tape is level) and snugly measure the fullest part of your hip — usually 7"-9" from waist. Wear underwear you normally wear with pants, since girdles and pantyhose can change the fit.

This also applies to buying patterns for straight skirts. Full pants and full skirt patterns may be purchased by waist size, since the waist would be the only area to fit.

Fill In:

My fullest hip measurement is: _____ in/cm

My waist measurement is: _____ in/cm

But I'm Between Sizes!

If you are between sizes, select the smaller size. Pattern companies add at least 2" ease to body measurements. If you are 39" in the hips and buy a 38" hip (size 14), you'll get 40" in the pattern. Letting out the side seams just ¼" would give you 1" more room which should be quite comfortable. If you buy a 40" hip (size 16), the pattern will measure 42" or 3" larger than your hips, which would probably be too full in hips, waist, and legs.

Chart from McCall's Patterns catalog
(All pattern company charts are the same)

Size	6	8	10	12	14	16	18	20	22	24
Bust	30½	31½	32½	34	36	38	40	42	44	46
Waist	23	24	25	26½	28	30	32	34	37	39
Hip	32½	33½	34½	36	38	40	42	44	46	48
Back Waist Length	15½	15¾	16	16¼	16½	16¾	17	17¼	17⅜	17½

But I'm 3 Different Sizes on the Bottom!

Experimenting is the only way you'll find out which is the easiest size for you to work with. Pati is a size 12 waist, 10 crotch depth, and 14 hip. After trying all 3 sizes, she found the 12 easiest to use The 14 was too long in the crotch, too large in the waist, and the legs were too wide. The 10 required adding 4-6" in width. The 12 was the best compromise.

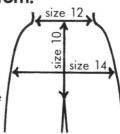

size 12

size 10

size 14

But My Top and Bottom are Different Sizes

Buy coordinates patterns to fit your top, then cut the bottoms wide enough to go around you! The top is much harder to alter. 70% of those attending our pant seminars are one size on top and another on the bottom. If this is your problem, make a basic pant fitting pattern in both your bottom and your coordinates sizes so you will learn exactly what to do with either size. Then you can use coordinates patterns with confidence!

Changing pattern sizes doesn't affect your alterations very much because when patterns are "graded", the largest change is in width (approximately 2" between sizes). If you have a flat derriere or "thighus gigantus" you'll have to make those adjustments in any size.

But the Pattern Doesn't Come in My Size!

If you understand how pattern companies "grade" their patterns, you will be able to create any size from the closest size available. Pattern companies make each size larger by spreading the pattern in approximately the amounts shown in the illustration. (Since this is only one leg, multiply all width adjustments by 4.)

Instant "Grading"

A simple way to grade a pant to your size is to buy a pattern close to your size and add or subtract in these places:

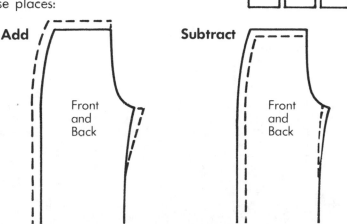

Add

Front and Back

Subtract

Front and Back

19

Slide Method of Adjusting Width and Length While Cutting

This is a simple way to make a size 10 coordinates pattern fit a size 14 bottom!

Determine how much width you need to add. If your hips are 39", you will need 41" (39" + 2" ease). If the pattern measures 40" you will need to add 1" total width. Since you will be adding to all 4 side seam allowances evenly, divide 4 into 1" — then add ¼" to the side seams when you cut. Always add or subtract same amount to side front and back. Never add to the center front or center back seams for width.

Make Pants Wider:

1. Pin pattern to fabric. Chalk mark amount to add.

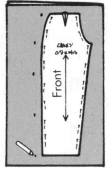

2. Cut all but side seam.

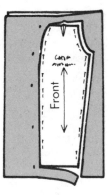

3. Unpin pattern. Slide pattern to chalk marks and cut side seam. Slide pattern back, mark darts.

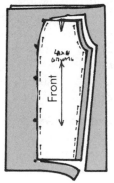

Make Pants Narrower:

Cut all but side, slide to marks, then cut side.

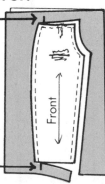

Make Pants Longer or Shorter:

Cut everything above knee, then slide pattern up or down to chalk marks. Cut pant lower edge.

See pg. 106 for using the slide method with trousers.

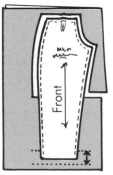

Do All Pattern Companies Fit the Same?

Pattern companies have standardized sizing because you can't try on a pattern before you buy it. If you have "thighus gigantus" with patterns from one pattern company, you'll have it in patterns from the others. However, even though they design from slopers that are similar in shape, the amount of ease added to the design varies with the look (pg. 17).

Don't Use Ready-to-Wear as a Guide to Your Size

The only size standards ready-to-wear manufacturers have is "the more you pay, the smaller size you'll fit into." Pati's size 14 derriere got into a size 8 Anne Klein pant that sold for $180. She almost bought them!! We call this vanity sizing! Ready-to-wear manufacturers don't have standards, because you can try on the merchandise before you buy it.

Some ready-to-wear manufacturers design their slopers for a young audience and some for a mature audience. Have you noticed that pants for the mature woman are fuller in the waist and flatter in the derriere? Pants for juniors are small in the waist and full in the derriere.

Proportioned Patterns

Proportioned patterns are not always the answer for a tall or short person. A short person can have very long legs! It is more important that you know **where** you are tall or short. Buy a **regular pattern** and lengthen or shorten it in the right places.

Finished Garment Measurements

We love patterns with finished garment measurements on the back of the pattern envelope! However, you need to know what ease you prefer.

If you buy a size 16, your hips measure between 40" and 42." A size 16 pant will vary in finished hip measurement, depending on style.

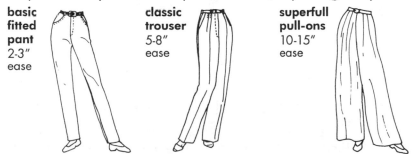

basic fitted pant 2-3" ease

classic trouser 5-8" ease

superfull pull-ons 10-15" ease

If you are short or heavy, you may choose to have no more than 8" ease in a full pant. You would buy the superfull pull-on pant 2 sizes smaller.

When you buy a pattern in a medium (12-14), it is cut for the size 14. Use the finished garment measurements to help you in deciding what size to buy.

A basic pattern is a simple style with a waistband, darts, center front or back zipper and a current, but classic, leg width. Most pattern companies offer a fitting basic drafted from the "sloper" (master pattern) which is used to design all their pant styles. Make a basic style pattern in gingham and alter it to fit. Make the same alterations on the tissue. The tissue then becomes **your own personalized basic pant pattern.**

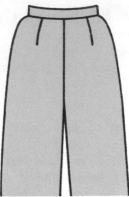

A basic pant style

Advantages of Fitting a Basic Pattern

The biggest advantage of all is that it will show you where your body varies from commercial patterns. Any alterations you make on the basic will automatically be made on any pattern before you cut. Your full tummy doesn't go away just because you switched from a Butterick to a McCall's pattern!

Once you fit the basic pattern to your body you can also:

1. Sew a basic pant style from it.

2. Use your basic to check length, width and crotch depth in other styles using the quick overlay method (pg. 50).

3. Design new details from the already fitted basic (pg. 58).

4. Try the altered gingham pant on once a year to see if your shape has changed. (Oh dear!)

Why Use Gingham?

1. The checks of woven gingham are built-in grainline markings, so you will instantly see fitting problems. When the horizontal checks are parallel to the floor and the vertical checks are perpendicular to the floor, your pants will look great!

2. The checks make pattern alterations easy. We recommend ¼" checks. After you've adjusted the gingham, just count the checks and you'll know the size of the adjustments you'll need to make on the pattern.

3. Gingham is lightweight enough to imitate knits, but also acts like a woven fabric because it is one.

Make an Adjustable Basic Pattern for Gingham

Use any commercial pattern for the gingham basic in a simple darted style but add these "in-case" seam allowances and a crotch depth outlet.

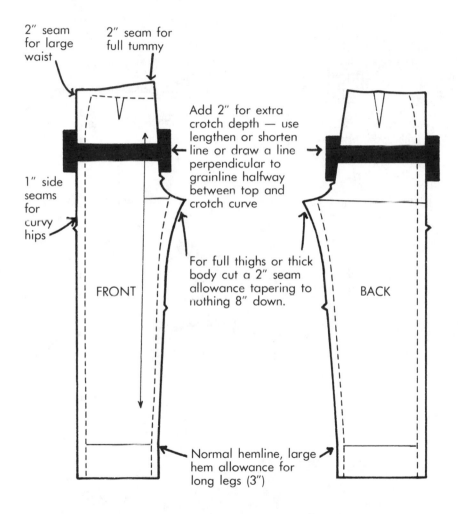

2" seam for large waist

2" seam for full tummy

Add 2" for extra crotch depth — use lengthen or shorten line or draw a line perpendicular to grainline halfway between top and crotch curve

1" side seams for curvy hips

For full thighs or thick body cut a 2" seam allowance tapering to nothing 8" down.

FRONT

BACK

Normal hemline, large hem allowance for long legs (3")

Or, an easier way . . . purchase a commercial pattern already designed with these larger seam allowances. Try the one we've designed for McCall's, #8173 available in sizes 6-22.

Sew the Gingham Basic Pant

1. Straighten gingham grain before cutting. Fold fabric lengthwise, matching selvages. If ends are not even, straighten fabric by taking short ends and pulling diagonally across the fabric until ends are even when fabric is folded lengthwise.

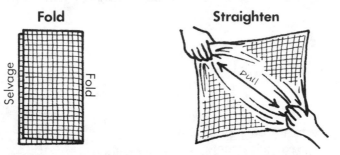

Fold

Selvage

Fold

Straighten

Pull

2. Cut gingham. Mark **every** stitching line with tracing paper so you will know how much you adjusted a seam.

3. Sew darts.

NOTE: Sew all seams with a long basting stitch for easy ripping.

4. Make tucks in front and back by bringing crotch depth outlet lines together. Make two more rows of stitching in tuck ¼" apart. (This makes lengthening the crotch easy — you just snip 1 row at a time.)

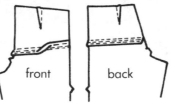

front   back

5. Stitch front to back at inseam.

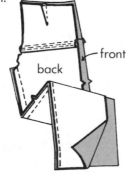

front

back

6. Stitch crotch leaving tucks and inseam allowances free, and allowing for a front opening.

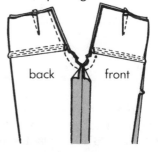

back   front

7. With wrong sides together, pin front to back at sides on stitching lines and pin up hem.

8. Try on right side out as your left and right sides may be different. Wear the same undergarments you plan to wear with your pants (pantyhose, girdle, etc.)

9. Tie ¼" elastic around your waist with lower edge of the elastic along waistline seam.

10. Be sure to try on with shoes you plan to wear with pants.

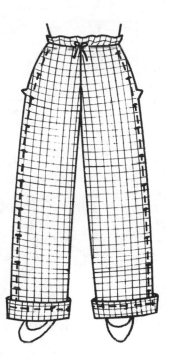

Now Fit

1. Read through all alterations in pgs. 27-37 first to become familiar with the process.

2. You can fit by yourself. The length of your own arm allows you to pin fit easily in hip and waist area without bending.

3. Stand in front of full length mirror with a hand mirror for back views.

4. After making alterations, always look to see if the change has affected another area. A change in the back can create a problem in the front.

5. The pant pattern curves at the sides may not match your curves. Ignore the pattern seam lines and pin the sides to fit YOU.

6. Chapter 6 shows you how to easily recognize fitting problems, whether you have many or few, how to adjust your gingham pant, and how to alter your pattern.

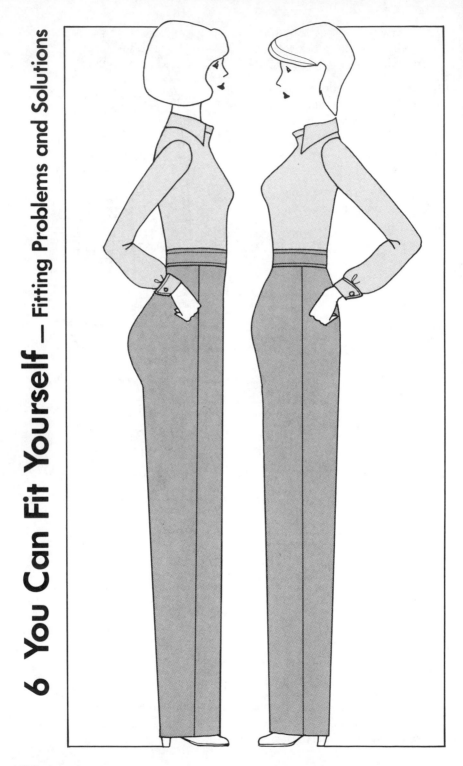

Now that you have your gingham pant, look at the checks, wrinkles, and side seams. They will identify your fit problem and we will tell you exactly what to do to solve the problem. (Gingham will not always be illustrated.)

LOOK AT:	PROBLEM	SOLUTION
Gingham Checks When vertical checks are perpendicular to floor, and crosswise checks are parallel to floor, you will have a good fit.	checks curve toward problem	let out inseam until checks fall straight
Wrinkles Usually point to fitting problem. A well-fitted pant has no wrinkles. Adjust until wrinkles disappear.	wrinkles point to problem	adjust until wrinkles disappear
Side Seams Can indicate center front and back problems that gingham and wrinkles may not show. Adjust at top until side seams are straight and centered in middle of leg.	side seam swings forward	adjust front and back at top until side seams hang straight

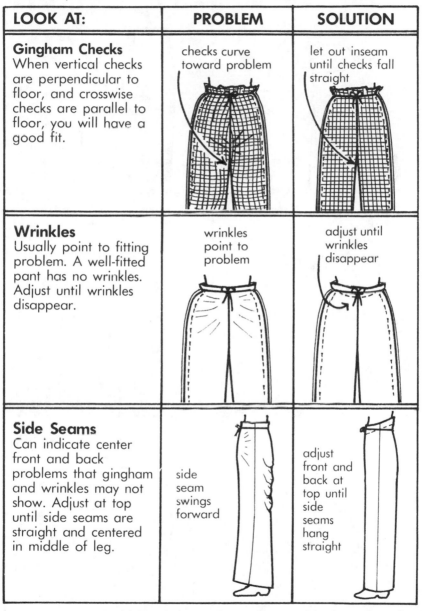

Correcting one problem can create another problem, so don't be afraid to go back and readjust any area. Read the whole chapter first so you'll know what to expect in fitting.

PROBLEM	SOLUTION
1. Horizontal wrinkles mean pants are too tight.	Let out side seams until wrinkles disappear. Add same amount to pattern.
2. Vertical wrinkles mean pants are too loose.	Take deeper side seams until wrinkles disappear. **NOTE:** Rather than altering pattern, pin fit side seams to your shape each time you sew.
3. Waist too tight, won't meet at center front.	Let out side seams at waist until center front comes together, or sew narrower darts (pg. 77). Add same amount to pattern Waist too loose, hips fine? Take deeper side seams in waist area.

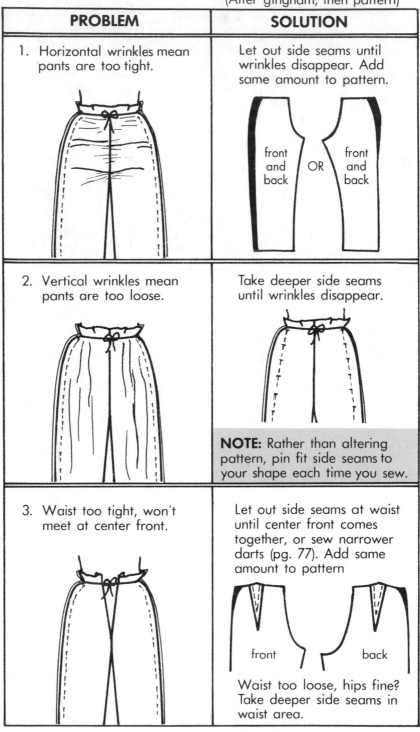

4. Crotch Depth: The distance from your waist to the bottom of your crotch.

Too short: touches crotch.
Too long: hangs down too far.

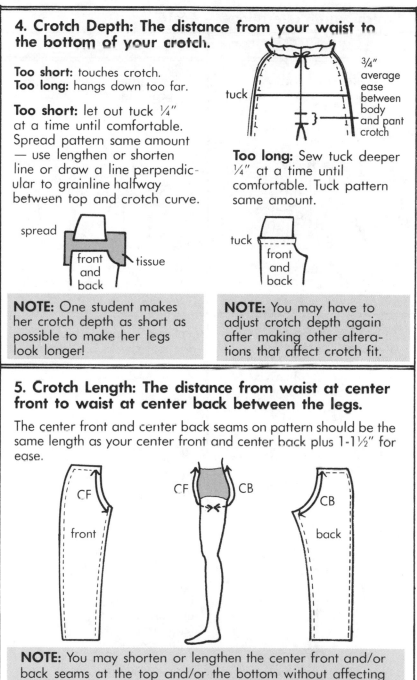

Too short: let out tuck ¼" at a time until comfortable. Spread pattern same amount — use lengthen or shorten line or draw a line perpendicular to grainline halfway between top and crotch curve.

¾" average ease between body and pant crotch

Too long: Sew tuck deeper ¼" at a time until comfortable. Tuck pattern same amount.

NOTE: One student makes her crotch depth as short as possible to make her legs look longer!

NOTE: You may have to adjust crotch depth again after making other alterations that affect crotch fit.

5. Crotch Length: The distance from waist at center front to waist at center back between the legs.

The center front and center back seams on pattern should be the same length as your center front and center back plus 1-1½" for ease.

NOTE: You may shorten or lengthen the center front and/or back seams at the top and/or the bottom without affecting crotch depth. A change in crotch depth does, however, affect crotch length. See problems #6-15 for crotch length alterations.

PROBLEM	SOLUTION

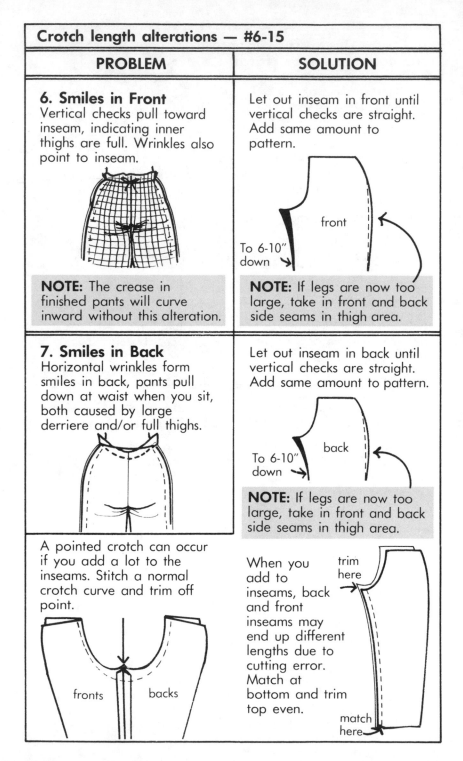

6. Smiles in Front

Vertical checks pull toward inseam, indicating inner thighs are full. Wrinkles also point to inseam.

SOLUTION: Let out inseam in front until vertical checks are straight. Add same amount to pattern.

To 6-10" down

front

NOTE: The crease in finished pants will curve inward without this alteration.

NOTE: If legs are now too large, take in front and back side seams in thigh area.

7. Smiles in Back

Horizontal wrinkles form smiles in back, pants pull down at waist when you sit, both caused by large derriere and/or full thighs.

Let out inseam in back until vertical checks are straight. Add same amount to pattern.

To 6-10" down

back

NOTE: If legs are now too large, take in front and back side seams in thigh area.

A pointed crotch can occur if you add a lot to the inseams. Stitch a normal crotch curve and trim off point.

fronts   backs

When you add to inseams, back and front inseams may end up different lengths due to cutting error. Match at bottom and trim top even.

trim here

match here

PROBLEM	SOLUTION

8. Frowns in Front or Back

Vertical wrinkles near inseam indicate thin thighs.

Sew deeper inseam in front or back until wrinkles and frowns disappear. Cut same amount off pattern.

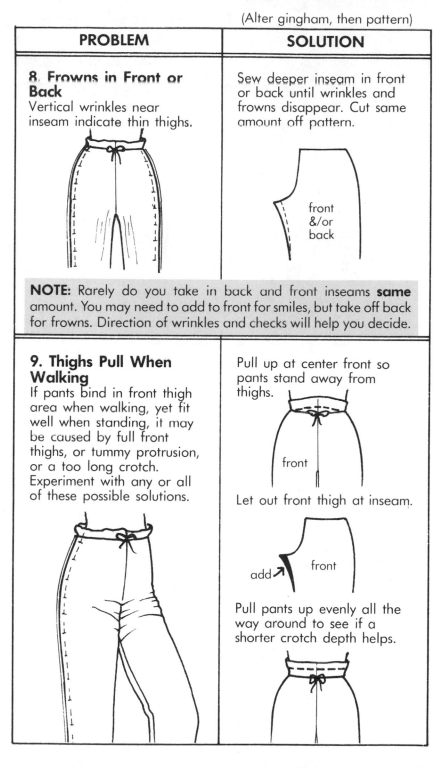

front
&/or
back

NOTE: Rarely do you take in back and front inseams **same** amount. You may need to add to front for smiles, but take off back for frowns. Direction of wrinkles and checks will help you decide.

9. Thighs Pull When Walking

If pants bind in front thigh area when walking, yet fit well when standing, it may be caused by full front thighs, or tummy protrusion, or a too long crotch. Experiment with any or all of these possible solutions.

Pull up at center front so pants stand away from thighs.

front

Let out front thigh at inseam.

add↗ front

Pull pants up evenly all the way around to see if a shorter crotch depth helps.

PROBLEM	SOLUTION

10. Sway Back
Wrinkles below waistband in back.

Pull pants up at center back until wrinkles are gone. Mark waist seam lower by same amount on pattern.

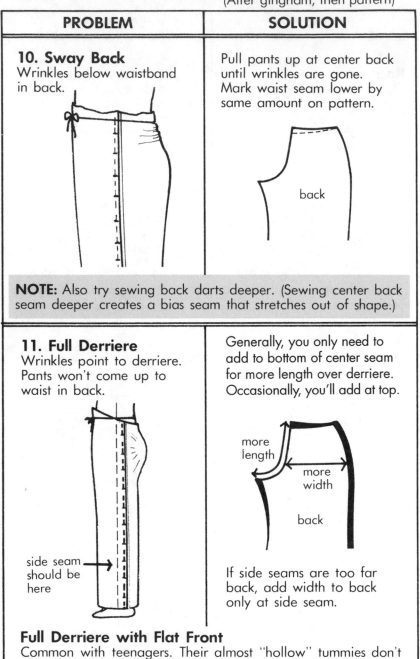

back

NOTE: Also try sewing back darts deeper. (Sewing center back seam deeper creates a bias seam that stretches out of shape.)

11. Full Derriere
Wrinkles point to derriere. Pants won't come up to waist in back.

Generally, you only need to add to bottom of center seam for more length over derriere. Occasionally, you'll add at top.

more length

more width

back

side seam should be here

If side seams are too far back, add width to back only at side seam.

Full Derriere with Flat Front
Common with teenagers. Their almost "hollow" tummies don't even need darts for shaping. Eliminate darts (pg. 78). Front pattern piece will be too wide making side seams too far back. If pants are tight, add to back side seams, if loose, take off front side seams until they are in proper position.

(Alter gingham, then pattern)

PROBLEM	SOLUTION

12. Flat Derriere
Bagginess in the back. (Very common in the over 30 age group when gravity begins to take its toll!)

Pull pants up at center back until wrinkles disappear. Mark new seam line on pattern. This may cause smiles in front, if so, let out front inseam.

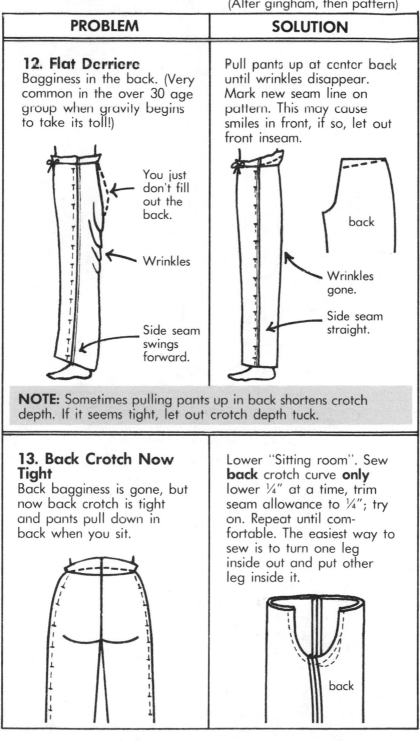

You just don't fill out the back.

Wrinkles

Side seam swings forward.

back

Wrinkles gone.

Side seam straight.

NOTE: Sometimes pulling pants up in back shortens crotch depth. If it seems tight, let out crotch depth tuck.

13. Back Crotch Now Tight
Back bagginess is gone, but now back crotch is tight and pants pull down in back when you sit.

Lower "Sitting room". Sew **back** crotch curve **only** lower ¼" at a time, trim seam allowance to ¼"; try on. Repeat until comfortable. The easiest way to sew is to turn one leg inside out and put other leg inside it.

back

33

PROBLEM	SOLUTION

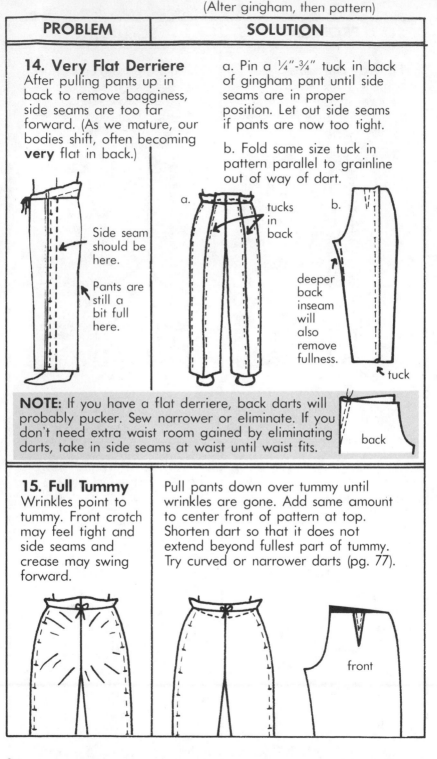

14. Very Flat Derriere

After pulling pants up in back to remove bagginess, side seams are too far forward. (As we mature, our bodies shift, often becoming **very** flat in back.)

a. Pin a ¼"-¾" tuck in back of gingham pant until side seams are in proper position. Let out side seams if pants are now too tight.

b. Fold same size tuck in pattern parallel to grainline out of way of dart.

Side seam should be here.

Pants are still a bit full here.

a.

tucks in back

b.

deeper back inseam will also remove fullness.

tuck

NOTE: If you have a flat derriere, back darts will probably pucker. Sew narrower or eliminate. If you don't need extra waist room gained by eliminating darts, take in side seams at waist until waist fits.

back

15. Full Tummy

Wrinkles point to tummy. Front crotch may feel tight and side seams and crease may swing forward.

Pull pants down over tummy until wrinkles are gone. Add same amount to center front of pattern at top. Shorten dart so that it does not extend beyond fullest part of tummy. Try curved or narrower darts (pg. 77).

front

34

PROBLEM	SOLUTION

16. Uneven Hips

A high hip can be caused by carrying babies, books, or grocery bags on one hip, by having one leg longer than the other, or by a spinal curvature.

Gingham checks slant upward on one side and one pant leg is shorter than the other. Diagonal wrinkles point to high side.	Easiest way to alter is to pull pants up on **low** side until checks are straight and pants level. If one thigh is also larger, let out inseams on both legs and take deeper side seam on smaller leg. You may also need to let out side seam on leg with larger thigh.

If crotch is now too tight, let out crotch depth tuck until comfortable. Alter pattern same amount.

Mark lower seamline on pattern as a reminder to lower waistband on one side when sewing pants.

Experimentation is the Key!

When you are not sure how to solve a problem, use the trial and error method. An adjustment in one area may affect another area and there may be more than one solution to a problem, for example:

Lengthening center seam length may make crotch more comfortable without adjusting crotch depth.

Lengthening crotch depth gives more crotch length over tummy and derriere.

Lengthening crotch depth may make thighs that were too tight suddenly comfortable OR make the back baggy. Take off crotch seam at top or bottom.

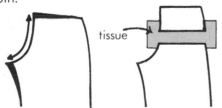

tissue

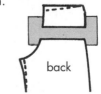

back

Combination Problems

Side seams are a clue! If they swing forward, it may be from a full tummy, flat derriere, and/or a slanted waistline (one that is high in front and low in back).

Pull pants down in front and up in back until side seams are straight.

Add same amount to center front at top of pattern and take off center back at top.

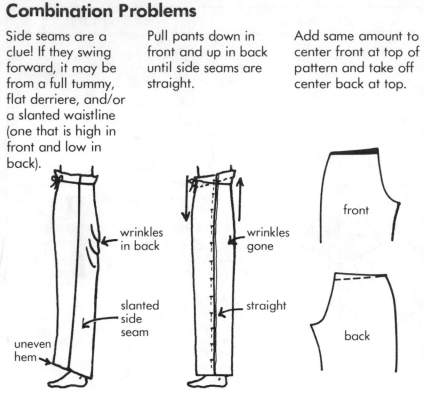

wrinkles in back

wrinkles gone

slanted side seam

straight

uneven hem

front

back

Make Pants More Flattering

The wrinkles may be gone, the checks and side seams straight, but you don't like pants on you because they emphasize your tummy or derriere. The narrower the legs in the thigh area, the more your tummy and derriere will be emphasized. If you are wearing long tops over pants, narrower legs may be more flattering. But when you want to tuck in a top, simply add to the inseam of front and/or back until pants fall more gradually from the fullest part of your body.

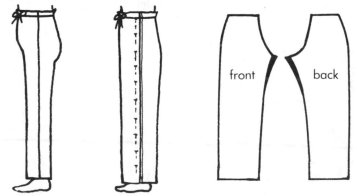

front

back

Crotch Curve Changes that Can Make Pants More Flattering

If you have a full tummy, straighten front crotch curve. You'll gain 1-1¼" in width across tummy.

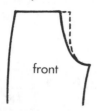

front

Eliminate smiles without making legs fuller. For extra length around your derriere, sew a more acute crotch curve instead of adding to inseam.

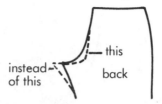

instead of this

this

back

Pant Length

Try pants on with shoe heel height you plan to wear with pants. Fold deeper or shallower hem. (pg. 25) Pants should hit top of your shoe and be same distance from floor all around. Mark finished length on pattern, allowing for a 1½"-2" hem.

Mark Changes on Gingham Basic Pant, Then on Pattern Tissue

Using chalk or a washable marking pen, mark below elastic while still wearing pants.

Unpin front opening. Take off pants. Open up side seam allowances and mark pin positions on wrong side.

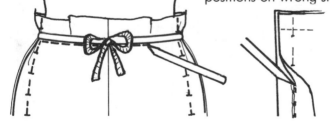

Two suggestions for transfering changes made on gingham pant to basic pattern tissue:

1. Measure difference between original seam line (tracing paper mark) and new seam (pen or chalk marks on gingham). Move seamline on pattern same amount. Use a nylon tip pen to draw new seam line on tissue pattern. Count ¼" gingham checks for easy measuring.

2. Unpin side seams. Place tissue on top of gingham. Trace side seams onto tissue. You undoubtedly will be shaped differently than pattern!

   We do not recommend totally unstitching gingham as one year from now you may want to try it on again to see if your body has shifted!

Summary of the Most Common Alterations

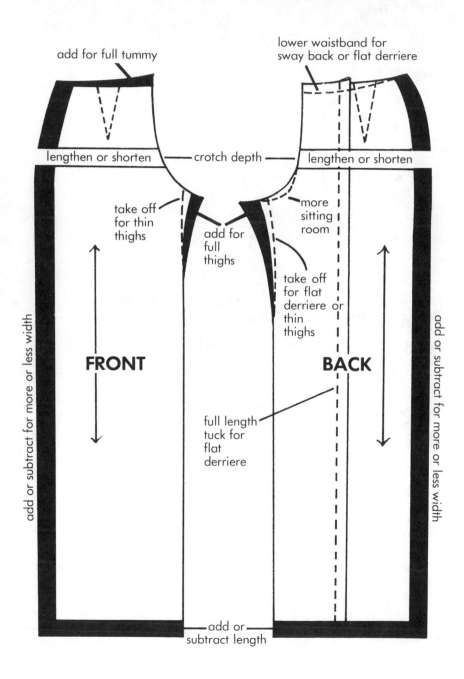

add for full tummy

lower waistband for sway back or flat derriere

lengthen or shorten — crotch depth — lengthen or shorten

take off for thin thighs

add for full thighs

more sitting room

take off for flat derriere or thin thighs

add or subtract for more or less width

FRONT

BACK

add or subtract for more or less width

full length tuck for flat derriere

add or subtract length

My Personal Pattern Alterations

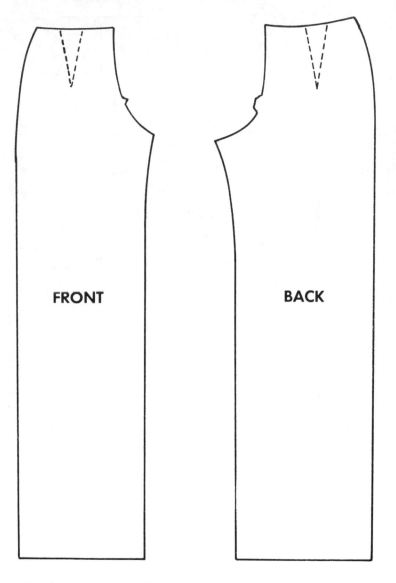

FRONT   BACK

1. Pattern number you are using for your basic _____ . Size _____ .

2. Make it up in gingham (pg. 22).

3. Fit, referring to "Fitting Problems and Solutions" (pgs. 27-37).

4. Summarize adjustments you made during fitting on this page. This will be a quick reference for the differences between your body and a commercial pattern.

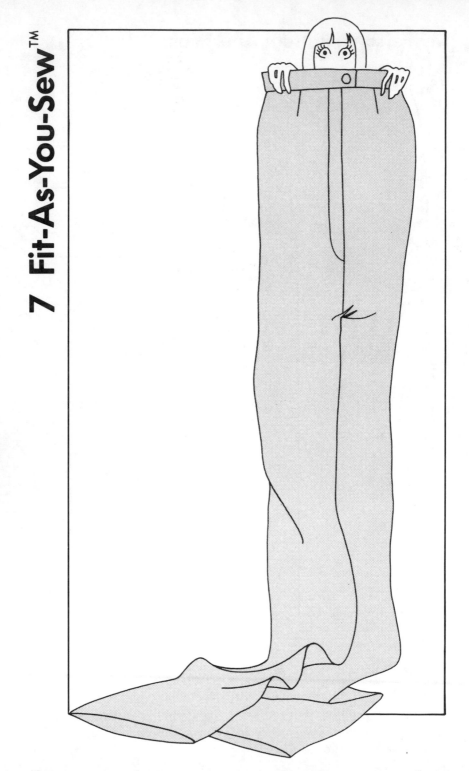

Fit-As-You Sew™

Whether you are using the "Easy way out" fit method or the "It takes a little longer, but it's sure worth it" way, the Palmer/ Pletsch **Fit-As-You-Sew™** system will be one of the most important steps to a good fit. Since our weight fluctuates (for some on a daily basis!), we use fabrics of varying weights and drapability, and we don't **always** cut **perfectly** accurately, **Fit-As-You-Sew™** still allows us to deal with these variables and sew perfectly fitted pants.

We always sew pants in just our underwear — then we are ready to try them on as many times as necessary (at least 3 times and usually more) without the dress/undress hassle.

These light duty fitting tips will solve 90% of all fit differences. If your problem seems to be different from these, you may be part of the 10% who requires adjustments in cutting — see the previous chapter "You Can Fit Yourself" for more information.

Sewing Order

1. Sew darts.

2. Sew crotch seam starting 1½" from inseam to zipper opening. Backstitch.

3. Sew zipper into pants.

4. Sew front and back legs together at inseam. (If you sew front legs together, you'll have a skirt!)

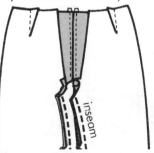

5. Finish sewing crotch seam from below zipper.

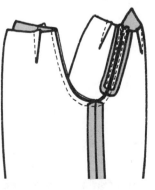

NOTE: If you have cut "in-case" seam allowances (pg. 14) use the snip mark method to mark original stitching lines, and sew to snips.

6. Lay pants flat and pin side seams with wrong sides together, spacing pins about 2" apart.

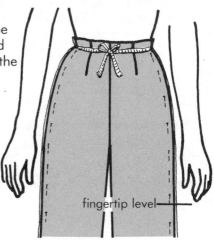

7. Try on **right side out** because your left and right sides may be different. Tie ¼" elastic around your waist with the bottom of the elastic on the waistline seam.

Now Fit

NOTE: You CAN fit yourself above fingertip level. You simply need two mirrors — a full length and a rear view mirror — so you don't distort the fit by twisting to see your back side.

fingertip level

After making any alterations, always look to see if the change has affected another area. A change in the back can create a problem in the front.

There are two areas where you need to adjust every pair of pants to get a perfect fit in any fabric, and it's so easy to do!

1. **Width**
   You will have horizontal wrinkles where pants are too tight. Pin shallower side seams in those areas until comfortable. Vertical wrinkles will appear where pants are too loose. Pin deeper side seam allowances in those areas until pants are comfortable.

   NOTE: Everyone is shaped differently at sides, so pin **your** pants to fit **your** shape at side seams.

2. **Crotch Depth**
   Only you know how comfortable the crotch feels. Technically, pants should hang down ¾" to 1" from your body in woven fabrics and ¼" to ½" in stretchy knits. (pg. 16).

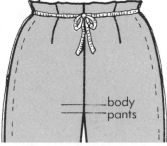

Raise pants to shorten crotch	**Lower pants to lengthen crotch**
If crotch feels too long, raise pants evenly all the way around under elastic until pants are comfortable.	If crotch feels too short, pull pants down evenly all the way around until crotch feels comfortable. (This is why we suggest cutting a 1" in-case seam allowance on top of pants.)

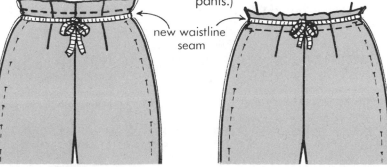

new waistline seam

3. **Smiles in Crotch**

Smiles indicate "thighus gigantus" (join the group — this is our problem too!) Let inseam out in back and/or front, depending on where smiles are, until wrinkles disappear.

Frowns in Crotch

Frowns indicate very thin thighs . . . lucky you! Sew deeper inseam in back and/or front, depending on where frowns are, until wrinkles disappear.

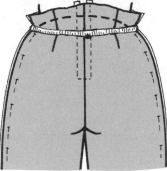

take in

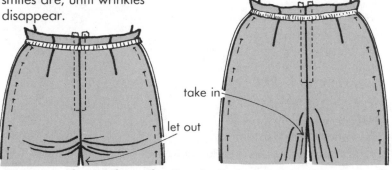

let out

4. **Baggy in the Back — Flat Derriere**

If pants are baggy in back, pull up at center back until wrinkles disappear. This often **creates** smiles in the front. If it does, let out front inseams.

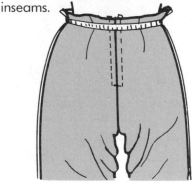

5. Ouch! Now you can't sit down. Pants have become too tight in back crotch. If front crotch seems long enough and **only** back feels tight, sew back crotch seam lower ¼" at a time, trim seam allowance to ¼" and try on. The easiest way is to turn one leg inside out and put the other leg inside it, then sitch.

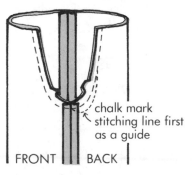

chalk mark
stitching line first
as a guide

FRONT   BACK

If front and back are **both** tight, since pulling up in back sometimes shortens entire crotch, pull pants down evenly all the way around until comfortable.

6. Sway Back

Horizontal wrinkles below back waistband means a sway back.

Pull up center back under elastic until wrinkles are gone.

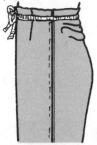

7. Full Tummy

If wrinkles point to the tummy . . .

Pull pants down at center front until wrinkles disappear.

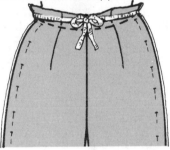

8. Uneven Hips

If wrinkles point to only one hip, and one pant leg is shorter, you have one high hip or one leg that's longer.

Pull pants down on the higher side until wrinkles disappear and hem is even. Note new waist seam on high side.

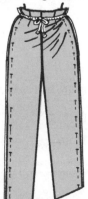
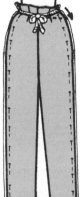

NOTE: If crotch is too long, pull pants **up on shorter side** instead.

Mark and Finish Pants

1. **Mark side seams and bottom of elastic.** Mark new waistline seam (bottom of elastic) while pant is still on your body. Take pants off and mark new side seams by spreading open side seams and marking on wrong side where pins join fabric.

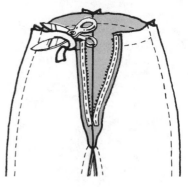

2. **Stitch side seams.** If you allowed an "in-case" seam allowance at top, trim to ⅝" so that it will be easier to attach waistband. You can leave larger side seam allowances, however, "in-case" you need them someday!

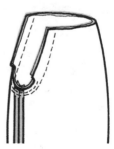

3. **Reinforce crotch seam** between notches by sewing another row of stitching ¼" from the seam line. Trim close to stitching.

NOTE: Never clip or snip the lower crotch curve. It isn't necessary and will weaken it.

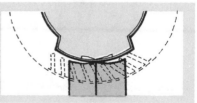

NOTE: Finish crotch so it will never rip out. Use stretch overlock stitch if your machine has one.

4. Pin waistband onto pants and try on. You may need to lower band a bit all the way around since elastic holds your pants tighter and higher than a waistband. You may notice these two common problems:

Wrinkles below band. This means pants are tight in high hip area.

Let side seams out in this area on both sides.

If you have a tummy bump, pants will droop in hollow area on either side of it. Sew band deeper here to remove wrinkles.

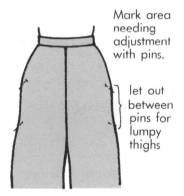

5. Sew on band (Chpt. 15, pgs. 87-92) and hem pants. Finished — and they FIT PERFECTLY!!!!!!

My Goodness, We Haven't Even Mentioned Ripping!!!

Mark area needing adjustment with pins.

If you really want perfect fitting pants, try them on 5-10 times while you sew to "fine tune" the fit. Even letting out a seam ⅛-¼" can make a major difference in fit . . . and that means **ripping**!!!!
For example, letting out side seams only ⅛" can camouflage lumpy thighs, because you'll get an extra ½" in width.

let out between pins for lumpy thighs

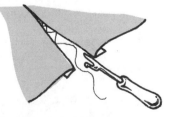

1. Cut stitches with a seam ripper every inch on one side of seam and pull thread on other side. Pull out or brush off clipped threads.

OR

2. Pull seam apart then carefully cut stitches. Don't use this method on fine silks or knits.

If you have altered a basic pattern to fit you and would like to use it to sew from, to design from, or to use for easy altering of other patterns, protect it! If you made a gingham pant from this pattern, save the pants too. You can try them on over the years to see if your shape has changed. Re-fit the gingham pants and transfer changes to the permanent pattern.

Method I (our favorite)

Iron a woven fusible interfacing (Shape-Flex® or Armo's P-91) onto the back of your pattern. Use a dry iron at a cotton setting, press for 10 seconds or longer in each spot for permanent bonding. With this method you will always be able to see what changes you have made in the commercial pattern.

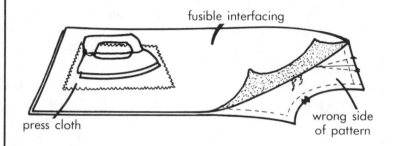

fusible interfacing

press cloth

wrong side
of pattern

Method II

Trace your pattern and all markings onto a medium weight non-woven interfacing. Use tracing paper and a smooth edge tracing wheel. Put cardboard underneath for more resilient surface for clear tracing paper markings.

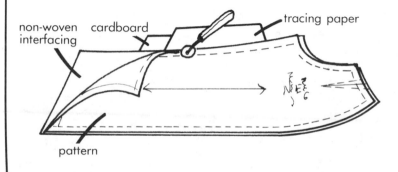

non-woven   cardboard   tracing paper
interfacing

pattern

Use Your Basic to Check Other Patterns

Once you have fitted your basic, you can use it to check the length and width (or ease) of new fashion pant patterns before cutting. Then, fine-tune the fit with **Fit-As-You-Sew**™.

1. Make same alterations on a new pattern that you made on your basic. If you alter for a full tummy in one pattern, you will have to alter for it in **all** patterns.

2. Place new pattern over basic. Line up crotch lines (a line from crotch seam intersection perpendicular to grainline on both front and back).

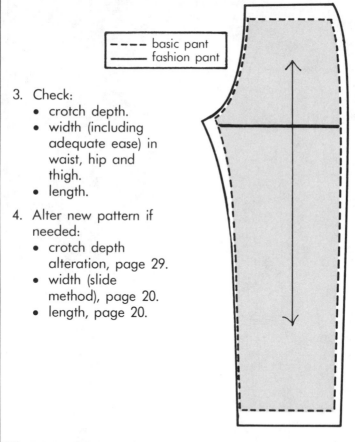

- - - - - basic pant
———— fashion pant

3. Check:
    - crotch depth.
    - width (including adequate ease) in waist, hip and thigh.
    - length.

4. Alter new pattern if needed:
    - crotch depth alteration, page 29.
    - width (slide method), page 20.
    - length, page 20.

But the patterns won't line up when I overlay!

True — that's why overlay can be only a method to check length and widths. If patterns weren't cut a bit differently, all pants would look alike!

If a style is larger than your basic, yet the sizes are the same, don't make the new pattern smaller! It might just be "design ease" (pg. 17). For example, the front of a trouser style is cut wider (so the pleats will lie flat) and longer in the crotch (for a more relaxed fit).

Sometimes the center front or back will be more slanted on one style than the other. To eliminate a dart, the designer usually slants the center seam to remove width normally taken up by sewing dart. If you **need** more room over the tummy, cut center front straight.

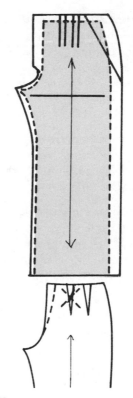

Turn Your Basic into a Pull-on Pant

Cut on a casing and use either elastic or a drawstring — an excellent finish if you want a waistline that gives when you do. Follow these simple steps:

1. Cut an extension above waistline seam on pant front and back twice the width of the elastic plus a seam allowance. For example, 1" elastic × 2 + ⅝" = 2⅝". Don't sew the darts.

NOTE: If your hips are very large compared to your waist, cut the side seams straight up so top of pant will be large enough to go over hips.

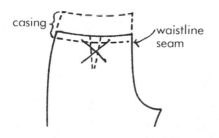

casing

waistline seam

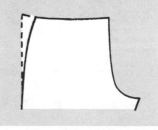

Sew Pull-On Pants in Any Fabric

Whether you use a favorite pull-on pant pattern or convert your basic to a pull-on, here's how to fit and sew them in the easiest, most flattering fashion.

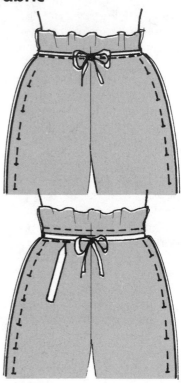

1. Sew inseams and crotch seams and pin side seams wrong sides together. Try on with ¼" elastic around your waist.

2. Pin fit deeper or shallower side seams and pull up or down evenly all the way around until crotch is comfortable. (pg. 43). Mark new waistline.

NOTE: Ease commonly needed:

	doubleknits	wovens
hip	1"	2"
crotch depth	¼"-½"	½"-¾"

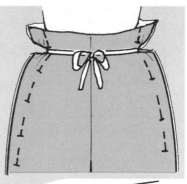

NOTE: Get rid of extra bulk at the waist by pinning side seams deeper at the top and then try to pull pants down over your hips. The amount of fullness you can eliminate depends on your shape and the give in the fabric. If you want a smooth fit instead of a more gathered "pull-on" appearance, try to fit as close to the body as possible, but remember they must "pull on and off."

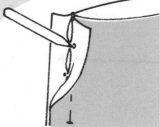

3. Take off and mark where pins are on wrong side. Unpin, place right sides together and sew on marks.

4. Trim seams in casing area to ¼" and fuse down with a strip of fusible web so the seams won't get in the way when threading elastic through casing.

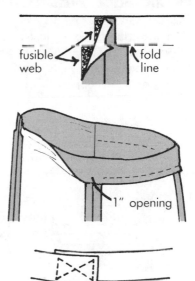

5. Fold casing to inside and top-stitch. Leave a 1" opening at center back through which elastic may be threaded.

6. Wrap elastic around your waist until snugly comfortable, add 1" to allow for a ½" overlap.

7. Thread elastic through casing and finish off ends by over-lapping ½" and stitching them together in an "X" as shown.

NOTE: Try Ban-Rol elastic (X-L 90 from Staple Sewing Aids). It will never wrinkle, roll or bend permanently in half.

Pull-On Pants with a Separate Casing

This method works best on knits because pants can be fitted smoothly at the waist and still have enough stretch to pull over hips. The casing also gives pull-on pants the fashion look of a waistband.

1. Make a waistband the same size as the top of the pants. Stitch as shown and fold wrong sides together.

2. Pin to outside of pants as shown.

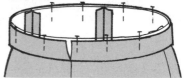

3. Stitch, trim seam to ⅜" and stitch or zig-zag all seam allowances together to make them flat.

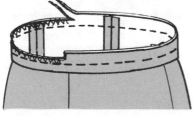

4. Thread elastic through opening. Pin ends together and try on to fit. Finish ends as above. (Or leave in pin for adjustability!!)

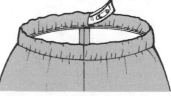

Elastic Back Waistband

This waistline treatment gives the trim look of a waistbanded pant in front, yet has the stretchy comfort of elastic in the back. Add a fly zipper extension to the front of your basic pant, (pg. 83) as this pant has a front opening.

1. Add extra fabric for casing to top of back pant piece and cut side straight up. Do not stitch darts.

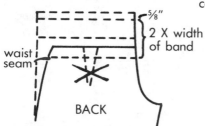

2. Stitch center back crotch seam. Finish top edge. Fold down casing and stitch.

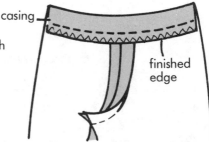

3. Cut, interface (pg. 87), and stitch waistband pieces to front.

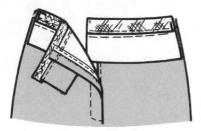

4. Insert elastic in back casing, pin elastic ends to anchor them. Pin front and back side seams together.

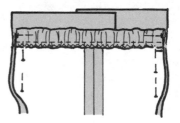

5. Try pants on to make sure waist is comfortable. Adjust elastic if necessary.

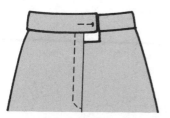

6. Sew side seams through waistband. Backstitch at top. Clip side seam allowances to seamline at waistline. Press allowances above waistline toward front.

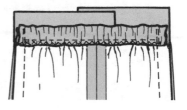

7. "Stitch-in-the-ditch" or the well of the seam from the right side to anchor front bands.

8. Slipstitch front ends of waistband and side seams. Stretch back waistband until smooth and stitch several rows of stitching through all layers.

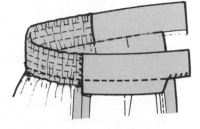

NOTE: You can even use this idea with your favorite trouser pattern.

The No-Side-Seam Pull-on Pant

This pant is great out of soft lightweight knits or silky wovens for evening or summer casual.

1. Make sure pattern measures 2" larger than body in the hip area, as you will have no side seam to let out. Lap front and back pattern pieces at sides. Leave out darts, cut on casing. (pg. 51)

2. Sew inseams. Press open.

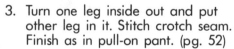

3. Turn one leg inside out and put other leg in it. Stitch crotch seam. Finish as in pull-on pant. (pg. 52)

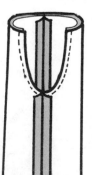

Turn Your Basic into a Faced Waistline Pant

This is a great finish for short-waisted people:

1. Fold darts of basic pattern.

2. Measure 3" down from top edge of pattern. This section will be facing pattern.

3. Cut facing, apply to waistline.

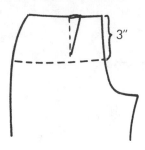

NOTE: Try interfacing the facing with a sheerweight fusible interfacing for more body. To prevent stretch at the top edge sew ¼" twill tape into seam when attaching facing to pants.

Drawstring Waistline Pants

1. Cut a 2" casing. Sew a buttonhole ½" from each side of the center front. Zigzag raw edge if ravelly. Trim seam allowances above fold line to ¼".

2. Fold casing to inside. Stitch ⅜" from the top edge and again ¾" from top. Thread ¼" drawstring or cording through casing.

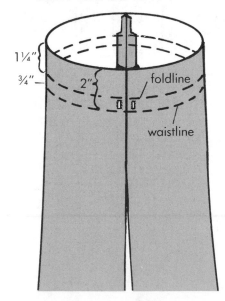

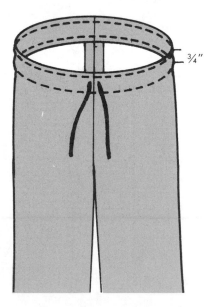

Create a Jogging Pant

Follow the instructions for elastic casings (pg. 53) or drawstrings (pg. 56) and add them to top and/or bottom of your basic pattern.

Quick Knickers

Cut off any pant or pattern and sew a casing at the bottom for instant knickers. Cut them at least 6" below bottom of knee to allow for casing and blousing if you need it.

Attach a Halter

Susan saw this clever jumpsuit/sashed pant in a resort boutique — now you can add it to any pant!

Cut a rectangle 84 x 10", with diagonal ends. Sew a narrow hem. Attach to front waistline seam of any back zip pant.

Wrap to the back and then to the front and tie for a halter.

Or, just wrap it around the waist for a wide sash that stays in place over a tucked in blouse.

Add Design Lines

If you would like to make minor design changes or create a look you can't find in the pattern books, it's as easy as drawing a line! Create any design line by cutting the pattern and adding seam allowances. Sew the new seam and you have an instant design line.

Vertical Seaming

For pants that form-fit your derriere (great if you are flat in back). Cut through center of dart to hemline. Add seam allowances.

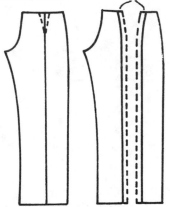

Design A Yoke

Draw a straight or curved line. Fold dart out of yoke before cutting fabric, add seam allowances.

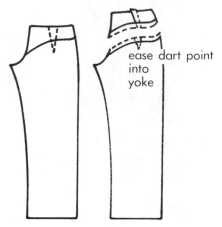

ease dart point into yoke

Knee Seaming

Draw an upside down "V" at knee in front and back. (great for leather and suede — real or synthetic). Add seam allowances.

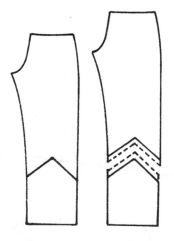

Color Splicing

A fun idea for summer cottons, evening pants, jeans and children's clothes. Cut pattern, add seam allowances. Cut sections out of various colors of fabrics.

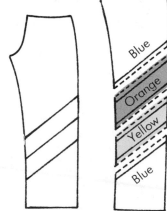

Blue
Orange
Yellow
Blue

Change Leg Width of Your Basic (Or Other Pants!)

A straight leg pant (18-21" at bottom) is universally flattering. Try on the pants and if you don't like the width, experiment by re-pinning width, and/or trying different lengths and styles of tops with the pants.

Make Pattern Wider or Narrower When Cutting

Tape extra tissue to inseams and outseams. Mark an equal amount to be added to inseam and outseam at hem. From fingertip level on outseam, and slightly lower on the inseam, draw new cutting lines using a yardstick as a guide.

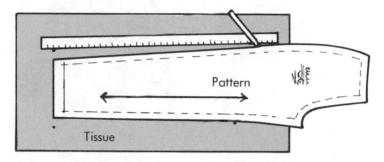

Make Pants Wider or Narrower When Sewing or Altering

The best way to see if you like the look of narrower legs is to pin the inseams and outseams narrower and try them on. Look in the mirror to see if you like the new width. If so, that's where you sew!

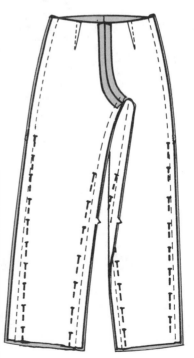

NOTE: Generally, begin at finger tip level on the outseam and lower on the inseam. If your inner legs are **very** thin, begin high on both. If inner legs are heavy, start at or below knee on inseam. The inseam and outseam should be taken in the same amount at the bottom.

Good Pant Fabrics

Woven Fabrics — stretch and non-stretch

Trigger® — 45" wide polyester/cotton fabric from Burlington/Klopman. Has a permanent press and soil-release finish. Due to a tight, firm weave, Trigger is hard to fit unless sewed in looser styles. Avoid it for your first pair of pants, but try it later for casual pants, children's or summer sportswear. Very washable.

Linen — Pants will be more wrinkle resistant if lined, underlined or worn with a pants liner. Looser trouser styling is also best for less wrinkling. Linen wears like iron — never pills — is worth its price. Dry clean. (Washable, but who wants to iron it!)

Synthetic Linens — 100% rayon or a blend of either rayon or linen with polyester. Washable, however washing can cause some loss of body so we prefer drycleaning. We have found that some pill with wear. Ask your store for a track record on the one you've chosen to buy.

Imitation Linens — Different from "synthetic linens," these are fabrics that are less expensive, washable, tighter in weave with a permanent press finish, usually a blend of cotton or rayon and polyester, and they wrinkle less. They have more of a sportswear look than a sophisticated linen look. Kettle Cloth by Concord is an example.

Stretch-Woven Polyesters — Fabrics woven with texturized polyester yarns. They can look like gabardines, linen, silk, and when blended with cotton produce stretch denim. Buy for their wrinkle resistance and comfort "give." Washable.

Denim — Most denim is 100% cotton. 14-16 ounce, but Dan River makes a wonderful 6-7 ounce denim that's great for summer wear. Don't straighten grain on denim. It has a mind of its own.

Chino — Chino is a sateen surface combed cotton sportswear fabric. It is best drycleaned as it will lose its shine and body if washed. Poly/cotton blended versions are washable.

Wool Gabardine — Wears extremely well. Many new lightweight gabardines are seasonless and don't need to be lined or underlined. They hold their shape beautifully and wrinkles just fall out.

Wool Flannel — Underline or line for wrinkle resist.

Lightweight Silky Wovens — Great for full, flowy evening pants and tops too. Silk is luxurious. There are also some wonderful polyesters that drape beautifully.

Silk Suitings — Luxurious pants. Line for better wear and less wrinkling.

Knit Fabrics — stretch and non-stretch

Stabilized Knits — Many knits today have little or no stretch and can be single or doubleknits. Pull on both directions to see if the fabric gives. They need as much ease as wovens for comfort.

Polyester Doubleknits — Require less comfort ease than wovens, sew easily and shape to the body for nice fit. They are washable and wear better than almost any pant fabric.

Wool Doubleknits — Easy to sew and lighter in weight than they were 20 years ago.

Interlock Knits — Great for evening or soft pant looks. They will run in one direction like a nylon stocking, but stay-stitching the edge that runs will prevent this.

Lycra® Blend Cotton Knits — When Lycra (a type of spandex fiber) is added, a fabric will have comfort, stretch and good stretch recovery. This will allow a tighter fit and more comfort in jeans, for instance. Cotton/Lycra is ideal for leggings. We've also seen wool/lycra gabardine.

Napped Fabrics — stretch and non-stretch

Velours and Sweatshirt Fabrics — Great for jogging pants and warm-up suits. Have lots of stretch, but are usually fitted looser due to end use. Washable.

Corduroy — Buy the best quality possible. Choose narrow-wale corduroy for less bulk and better wear.

Synthetic Suedes — Ultrasuede® Light makes lovely culottes and pants. Pants with soft fullness are nicest.

Real Suede and Leather — Very durable, comfortable to wear, usually lined to prevent knee and derriere stretch. Since these are sold by skins, not by the yard, knee seaming and yokes to piece skins are common (pg. 58).

How Can I Tell If a Fabric Will Make Nice Pants?

1. Will it wrinkle?

Perform the wrinkle test by holding a 5" square in your hand and squeezing it for five seconds. Do the wrinkles come out quickly? The higher the natural fiber content, the more it will wrinkle. Wovens wrinkle more than knits. Stretch wovens wrinkle less than regular wovens. Expect pants to wrinkle a bit where your body bends — knees and hips — but minimize wrinkles by testing fabric first.

NOTE: Learn how to sit in pants! Take a lesson from men. Pull up on the front of your pants at the knees before sitting. This prevents pants from pulling down in back, and minimizes baggy knees. It also lessens wrinkling in the front, because softer folds will form when you sit.

2. Will it hold its shape?

The "thumb test" is taken by pulling on a small section of the fabric with your thumbs and holding for five seconds. It if recovers quickly from the warmth and stress of your thumbs, it will hold its shape in wear. The tighter the knit or weave, the heavier the fabric, and the less absorbent the fiber, the better it will hold its shape. Generally, double knits hold their shape better than single knits, wovens better than knits and synthetics better than natural fibers. A fabric that fails the "thumb test" will leave you with baggy knees and derriere.

3. Will it pill?

The shorter the fibers, (fuzzy surfaces) the more it is likely to pill. The higher the synthetic fiber content, the drier and more static-prone it will be and thus the short fibers will cling together, or "pill", more easily. Pants will pill in the thigh area between the legs.

4. Will it sew easily?

Knits don't ravel, so seam finishes are unnecessary. Very stretchy fabrics may be harder to handle as well as fabrics made from slippery yarns. Synthetic fibers and fabrics with permanent press finishes may not press as easily as natural fibers.

5. Will it be comfortable?

Fabrics that are lightweight and high in natural fiber content are often more comfortable to wear. Thick knits and synthetics are often warm and feel clammy. However, they wrinkle less.

What Fabric Should I Use for My First Pair?

Our favorites are wool gabardine (expensive), stretch-woven polyester gabardine (inexpensive), and rayon or poly/rayon gabardine. Gabardine sews easily. It hangs beautifully on the body and wears better than many fabrics. Our wool gabardine pants cost between $30 and $50 to sew versus $90-200 to buy ready-made (truly a saving!) and they wear forever.

Yardage to Buy for Pants

Lay your favorite patterns on a 45" wide and on a 60" wide piece of fabric. Make a note of the amount of fabric you need for each. It will depend on your height and size as well as the style of your pants.

Make a card like this to carry with you. We need twice our length for plain pants from 45" fabric plus hem and waistband. This works even for napped fabrics since all pieces are cut in one direction. We need one length for plain pants from 60" fabric, plus hem and waistband. Trouser pants or pants with any pocket detailing may take additional fabric.

Yardage for pants	
plain	trouser
45" _____	_____
60" _____	_____

Do I Need a Special Pattern for Knit Fabrics?

If you use our **"Fit-As-You-Sew"**™'' system to fine tune fit in your pants, you can use any pattern for knit fabrics. A pattern that is designed ''for stretch knits only'' has less ease than a pattern cut for all fabrics, so just fitting the knit pant a bit tighter will accomplish what the ''for knits only'' pattern would do. But use caution — that tighter fit is more revealing and some bodies are best when hidden!

Wash or Dryclean?

Once you buy your fabric, you need to decide the method of care. Be sure to read the board end label as you will learn a lot about the fabric as this sample shows:

Burlington *klopman*	BANDMASTER®
	65% Dacron® polyester • 35% Combed cotton
⚠ 3 MACHINE WASH — WARM TUMBLE DRY LOW — REMOVE PROMPTLY USE COOL IRON IF NECESSARY	PERMANENT PRESS
	FABRIC PERFORMANCE GUARANTEED—SEE OTHER END

Fabric Care Guide

1. Read the bolt-end label for fiber and care information.

2. Preshrink your fabric, zippers, interfacings, and linings as you plan to wash or care for the finished garment. You may wash them all together — place zippers, tapes, and trims in a mesh laundry bag (available in hosiery departments).

3. Preshrink in the same manner you would wash:

   • Don't overcrowd washing machine
   • Use detergent when preshrinking
   • Use a cool rinse with synthetic fibers to minimize wrinkling
   • Take clothes out of washer and dryer immediately to prevent wrinkling
   • Don't over dry or you will create electricity and progressive shrinkage

4. Preshrink fabric to be drycleaned by having the drycleaner steam the fabric, or steam it yourself with a "shot-of-steam" type iron. Place fabric on bed, hold iron above fabric and slowly and thoroughly steam every inch. Allow to cool and dry before moving.

Notions to Make Your Sewing Faster

1. Cutting board — the folding cardboard variety has 1" ruled lines for ease in "squaring" fabric before cutting. OR, make a "Cut and Press" board, page 72.

2. See-through ruler — for placing pattern onto fabric on grain.

3. Tape measure — reinforced fiberglass won't stretch with use.

4. 7"-8" bent handled shears — (in good sharp condition). They glide under fabric to make smooth cutting easier.

5. Washable tracing paper — page 69.

6. Washable marking pen — the ink is water soluble. Be sure to read the directions!

7. Tailor's chalk in holder — for marking dry clean only fabrics. Look for the holder with a built-in sharpener.

8. Sobo Glue — a fabric glue for attaching underlinings.

9. Basting tape — a double-faced tape used in place of pins or hand basting.

10. 1/4" elastic — to hold pants up around waist while you fit.

11. A full length mirror and a hand held rear view mirror. Place in your sewing room and save fitting time.

12. Seam ripper — the best friend flattering pants can have!

13. Seam Sealant — a clear plastic liquid used on fabric raw edges to prevent raveling. Fray Check™ was the first.

14. Sta-Tape™ — for taping trouser pocket edges.

15. Steam iron — we like the "shot-of-steam" type irons for faster, better pressing.

16. Pressing equipment — see pressing chapter.

17. Serger — an overlock machine finishes edges of seam allowances quickly and neatly.

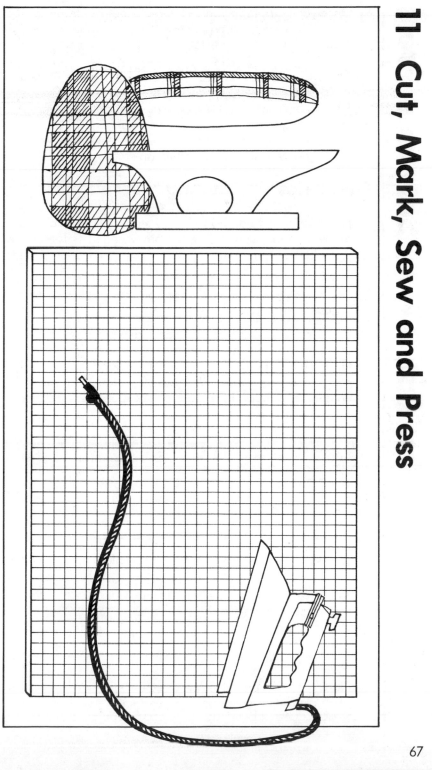

1. Once you learn to fit yourself, make 5 pairs of pants in one month! Concentrated practice will make sewing and fitting pants easier.

2. Use a pattern more than once. It gets faster each time.

3. You should be able to sew one pair in 3 hours and 2 pairs in 4 hours. Sewing 2 pairs at one time adds only 1 hour to the total sewing time. That's because repetition turns your sewing room into a mini-factory. Press a seam and while it cools, sew a seam on the other pair.

Quick Tips . . . Cutting

1. Fold fabric right sides together so seams will be in a ready-to-sew position. Can't tell right from wrong side? Then there probably isn't one. Most fabrics come folded right sides together.

2. Use a see-through type ruler for placing pattern on fabric grain.

3. Use a cutting board so you can place pins vertically into board in every corner of fabric. Angle them slightly toward the center so pattern won't slip. Your hands can be extra pins. Keep one hand on edges of pattern while cutting. Practice by cutting slowly at first, but soon this will become a real time saver!

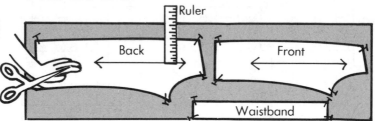

4. Cut **IN-CASE** seam allowances in problem areas (see pg. 14). It's like having an "in-case" dinner in the freezer. Do this when you are not quite sure how a design will fit or you are using a heavier fabric that might need more room.

5. Cut waistband on selvage to eliminate finishing and to allow you to use faster "stitch-in-the-ditch" technique (pg. 90).

6. Placing pattern pieces in one direction eliminates possibility of shading differences or "nap" effect of some of today's fabrics.

Quick Tips . . . Marking

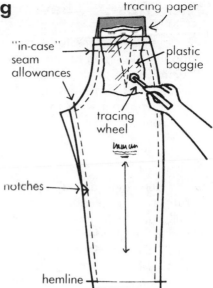

1. Snip mark for speed and accuracy when cutting. Cut off notches and snip ¼" into cut edge through center of remaining notch. Also snip hemlines, unusual seam allowance intersections, and tops of tucks.

2. Use tracing wheel and washable tracing paper. Protect pattern by placing a plastic baggie over it before tracing.

3. On fabrics where tracing paper doesn't show, place pins through the dart points vertically, lift the pattern off and mark with washable marker or tailors chalk on wrong side where pins penetrate fabric.

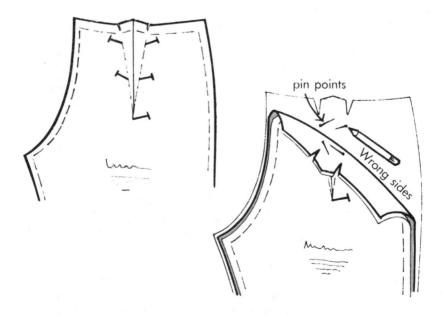

Quick Tips . . . Sewing

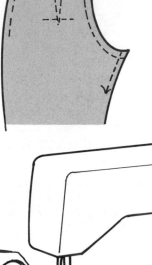

1. Is staystitching necessary? Yes! You will be trying on pants several times so staystitch any slightly bias edges directionally as shown, from wide to narrow, ½" from the edge.

2. Use our "taut sewing" technique to prevent puckering of seams. Pull equally on fabric in front and back of needle as you stitch. Do not stretch, just pull taut as if you were sewing with your fabric in an embroidery hoop. Let fabric feed through the machine on its own. For knits, stretch seams a little or you will get puckering on the lower legs since knit fabric will have more give than thread.

3. Prevent "scooting" — the upper layer often scoots forward when sewing. The length of leg seams multiplies the effect. Prevent it by using lots of pins. If you begin to see a bubble, lift the take-up lever to raise the presser foot just a hair. Place fingers of your right hand on both sides of the presser foot to help excess fabric feed into seam. Using a lighter presser foot pressure prevents scooting, too.

4. Backstitch ⅝" into seam at intersection points instead of at edge. For example, as you trim crotch seam you accidentally trim off backstitching done at edge, creating a weak point.

backstitch ⅝" down from top

70

Easy Seam Finishes

1. **None** — a seam finish may not be necessary when you plan to dryclean a fabric that doesn't ravel easily like many wool flannels, especially if you have lined them.

2. **Pinking** — is best for moderately ravelly fabrics you plan to dryclean or hand wash. When pinking, hold the blades loosely, because squeezing them will chew your fabric.

3. **Zigzagging** — a fast durable machine finish for medium and heavy weight fabrics, but will bunch up the edge of lightweight fabrics.

4. **Triple zigzag or serpentine stitch** — excellent for lightweight silky fabrics. Used with taut sewing (pg. 70) it will not pucker up the edges.

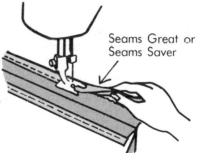

5. **Fray Check**™ — this clear liquid seals ravelly edges — is best for light to medium weight woven fabrics and silkies. Lightly apply to all edges while fabric is still on the cutting board. Dries in 5 minutes, will not wash or dry clean out, softens after cleaning. Rubbing alcohol will remove "ooops" spots.

6. **Seams Great**™ **or Seams Saver** — lightweight precut strips of nylon tricot that completely enclose the raw edges of **very** ravelly fabrics. Fold over seam and pull slightly taut so it wraps over seam edge and stitch. Use low iron temperature when pressing seams.

Seams Great or Seams Saver

7. **¼" seam** — perfect for loosely fitted pants out of velours, sweatshirt fabrics or lightweight knits. (Will not press-flat over your tummy or hips in doubleknits). Press seam in one direction.

Sew ¼" away and trim to **OR** Sew ¼" seam using the stretch
stitching.   overlock or a similar machine
                              stretch stitch. Trim to stitching.

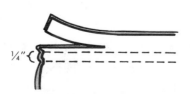

Speed Up Your Cutting and Pressing

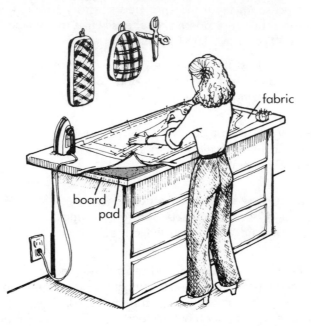

Make a "Cut and Press" board and get all of these benefits:

— You can pin straight into its padded surface.

— Place it on top of a chest for "elbow level cutting" — no more "seamsters backache!"

— It's a space saver — a dual purpose cutting and pressing surface that you can leave out all the time.

— The large surface makes easier fusing of interfacing to fabric as you can lay out all pieces to be fused at one time. Use it for creasing of pants too.

Materials:

— ½" thick particle board (plywood will warp). It should be long enough to cut out a pant length and wide enough for 60" fabric folded in half. (Ours is 32" x 48" — a third of a 4' x 8' sheet of particle board).

— ½" absorbent padding (old wool army blankets or rayon/wool felted carpet padding).

— cover with muslin or medium colored 1" gingham checked fabric.

Place padding on board, wrap with fabric, and tape fabric to wrong side of board with masking tape.

Press As You Sew

Pressing Darts

1. Press dart flat first to flatten fold line, and to eliminate any puckering in seam line.

2. Press dart toward center over a curve on pressing ham that matches curve of dart (and your body!). Tuck paper under fold if necessary to prevent an indentation from showing on right side. Steam press.

3. Flatten dart, especially point area with a pounding block/clapper.

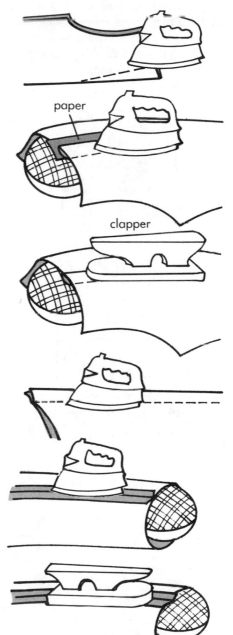

paper

clapper

Pressing Seams

1. Press seam flat first just as it was stitched to remove any puckers.

2. Press seams open over a seam roll to prevent "railroad tracks" or seam imprints from showing on right side.

3. While seam is still moist and warm, apply a pounding block. Use slight pressure for 5 seconds. The wood flattens seams better than pressing with the iron only, because it quickly absorbs heat and moisture.

4. Do not move pants until fabric is cool or what you have pressed in will fall out. Fabrics don't have a memory until they are cool.

Creasing Pants

A crease is a vertical line that makes anyone look thinner. It should go up to crotch level in the back, and just below the dart in front. In trousers, the front crease should meet the edge of one of the tucks, generally the one closest to center front. This gives a slimming vertical line from waist to toe.

plain pant   **trouser pant**

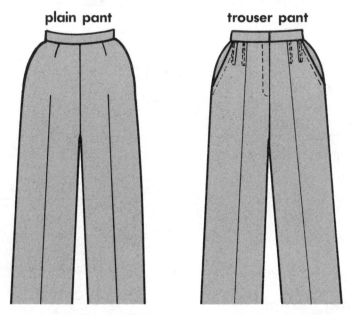

NOTE: Crease pants **after** they are finished because if the side seams are altered, the crease will move.

1. Place finished pants flat on pressing surface with inseams and outseams on top of each other. The crease should be in center of leg.

pounding block

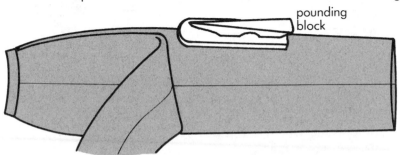

2. Press crease with an up and down motion of the iron so fabric won't stretch. Use a press cloth if fabric has a tendency to shine. Then place pounding block on edge to form a sharp crease.

Use this capsule sewing order for efficient pant sewing and fitting. Use your altered basic pattern or add 1" "in-case" seam allowances to new pattern to allow for minor adjustments. Sew pants in your underwear so you can try them on often to check fit! It's much easier to adjust as you go than to wait until pants are done.

1. Sew crotch seams from 1½" from inseam. Where there is a zipper, backstitch at opening.

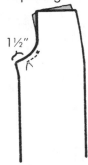

2. Sew darts, zipper, tucks, or pockets while pieces are flat. **Flat first is always faster.**

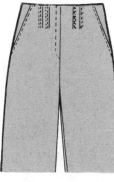

3. Sew back and front legs together at inseam. Lightly press open. (Don't sew the front legs together, or you'll have a skirt!!)

4. Finish sewing crotch seam.

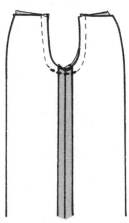

5. Pin side seams together, right sides out. Tie ¼" elastic around waist. Follow "Fit-As-You-Sew™" system, (pg. 41). Stitch, press.

6. Fit and apply waistband. Hem pants.

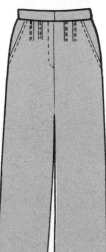

7. Done!

Sewing Darts

For a perfect dart without tying threads, stitch toward point, change to a shorter stitch length for the last ½", then stitch off the edge. Lift presser foot and pull dart toward you and stitch in the seam allowance to anchor chain.

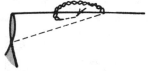

Fitting Darts

Darts are only markings placed on patterns by the pattern companies according to the shape of their perfect size 10 fitting model. If you are shaped differently, don't expect the darts to be right for you . . . change them!

Puckered Darts?

Front darts weren't made for most women over 30. We tend to have a bump in the tummy area that creates a hollow where the darts end. Darts point to bumps, if they point to a hollow they will pucker. Try one of the following:

Sew Narrower   **Sew Shorter**   **Sew narrower and shorter**

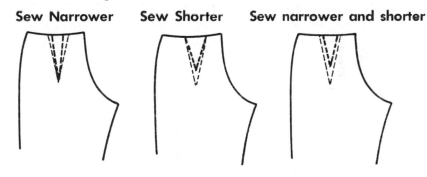

Small in the waist but full in the high hip and tummy?

Sew the dart curved to your shape rather than straight.

Flat Derriere and/or No Waistline?

Darts will pucker, as they are designed to point to bumps and curves. Leave out darts in front, in back, or both to gain waist room or to make pants straight like body.

Take in front **and** back side seams if waist is now too large.

If you've left out **only** the front (or back) darts, it may be necessary to take in **only** the side front (or back) to keep the side seams straight.

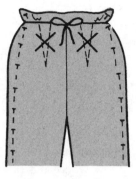

Convert Darts to Tucks or Gathers

Tucks and gathers are more flattering for many figures, because the soft fullness camouflages lumps and bumps. Try it in the back and/or front of pants. See page 103 for more on tucks.

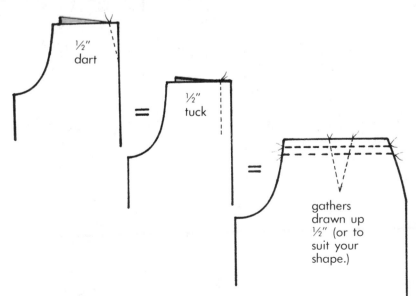

½" dart

=

½" tuck

=

gathers drawn up ½" (or to suit your shape.)

1. Buy a zipper 1-2" longer than you need! The slider won't get in your way and cause crooked topstitching. Sew in, then unzip zipper, sew band over top and cut off excess.

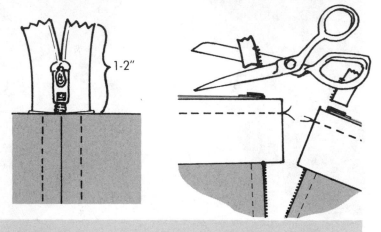

NOTE: Today's synthetic coil zippers are self-locking. They don't need to be zipped to the top to stay up. This means they are now shortened from the top, not the bottom.

2. Use a zipper that's long enough for you. A 9" works for most people, but use a shorter one if you are short in the crotch and a longer one if you are long in the crotch. If your waist is small and your hips large, you'll need a longer zipper.

3. Put zippers in center front or back even if the pattern calls for a side seam zipper because you can alter side seams without restitching the zipper.

4. Use these timesaving tapes: **Basting tape,** a narrow tape that's sticky on both sides used to eliminate hand basting. It comes on a reel covered with protective paper. Stick it to edges of zipper, peel away paper, and stick zipper to fabric. Stitch next to tape, not through it.

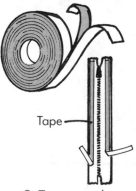

Tape

½" Scotch® Brand Magic Transparent® Tape, used as a straight topstitching guideline for both centered zippers (pg. 81) and lapped zippers (pg. 82).

Centered Zipper

1. Permanently stitch crotch seam 1½" from inseam to zipper opening. Backstitch. Machine baste seam closed. Break basting every 1-1½".

2. Press seam open. Place basting tape on right side of zipper edges. Center zipper coil over seam and stick in place.

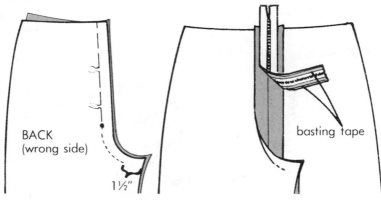

BACK
(wrong side)

1½"

basting tape

3. Center ½" Scotch tape over seam and topstitch along each side.

4. Remove basting tape. Remove Scotch tape and machine basting.

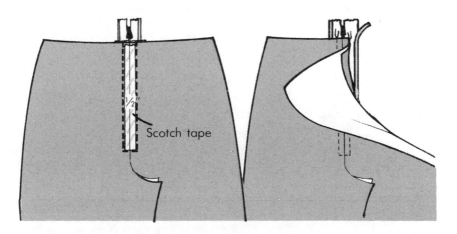

½"

Scotch tape

Lapped Zipper

1. Snip mark for zipper placement as shown. Permanently stitch crotch seam from 1½" from inseam to zipper opening. Backstitch.

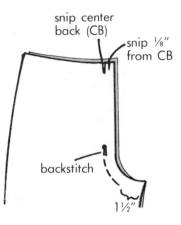

snip center back (CB)

snip ⅛" from CB

backstitch

1½"

2. Fold and press overlap and underlap.

Overlap side:
Press under ⅝" to crotch seam.

Underlap side:
Press under ½" (from second snip) creating a ⅛" underlap.

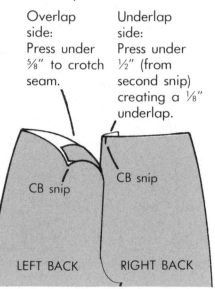

CB snip

CB snip

LEFT BACK   RIGHT BACK

3. Place basting tape on zipper and stick underlap fold next to zipper coil. Stitch close to fold with zipper foot. Place basting tape on overlap fold.

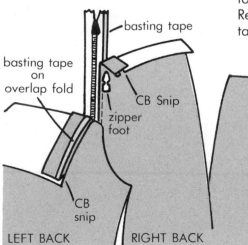

basting tape

basting tape on overlap fold

CB Snip

zipper foot

CB snip

LEFT BACK   RIGHT BACK

4. Stick overlap over zipper matching center back snips. Stick ½" Scotch Magic Tape next to fold, pin through all layers to prevent scooting, and topstitch next to tape. Remove basting and Scotch tape.

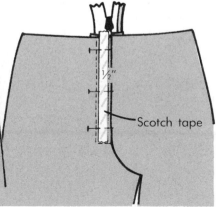

½"

Scotch tape

Fly Front Zipper

1. A fly front zipper is like a lapped zipper. A woman's fly laps right over left and a man's fly laps left over right (pg. 118).

   There is an overlap and an underlap. The fold line on the overlap side is the center front (CF).

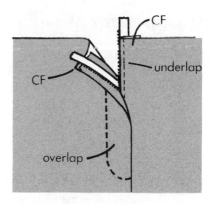

2. Check your pattern before cutting. The fly front extension should measure at least 1½" wide so it will be caught in topstitching.

If fly front is not 1½" wide, add width when cutting.

Add a fly front extension to any pant or skirt pattern. Just add on 1½" from CF line.

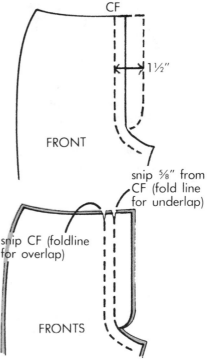

CF

1½"

FRONT

CF

1½"

FRONT

snip ⅝" from CF (fold line for underlap)

3. Snip mark fold lines for overlap and underlap. The overlap fold is the center front (CF). The underlap fold is ⅝" toward cut edge from center front and even with cut edge of crotch.

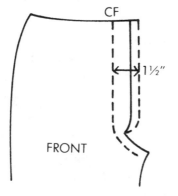

snip CF (foldline for overlap)

FRONTS

Fly Zipper for Women

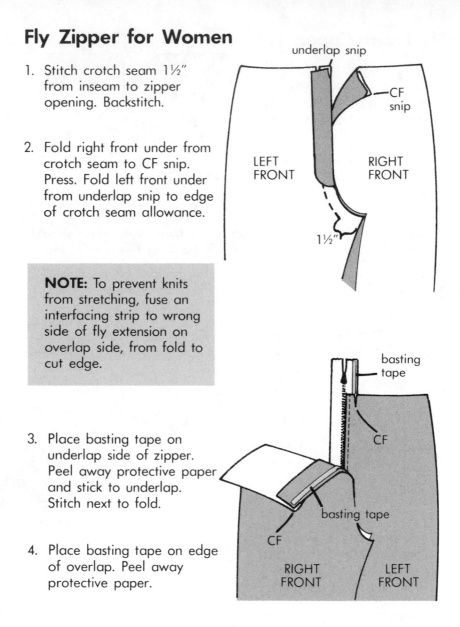

1. Stitch crotch seam 1½" from inseam to zipper opening. Backstitch.

2. Fold right front under from crotch seam to CF snip. Press. Fold left front under from underlap snip to edge of crotch seam allowance.

NOTE: To prevent knits from stretching, fuse an interfacing strip to wrong side of fly extension on overlap side, from fold to cut edge.

3. Place basting tape on underlap side of zipper. Peel away protective paper and stick to underlap. Stitch next to fold.

4. Place basting tape on edge of overlap. Peel away protective paper.

5. Line up CF snips and stick overlap in place.

6. Flip overlap out of way and pin zipper to extension only. Stitch zipper to extension from zipper side. (this is reinforcement stitching).

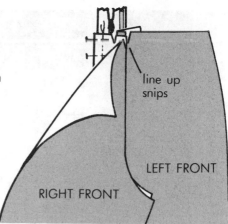

line up snips

LEFT FRONT

RIGHT FRONT

7. Lay fronts on flat surface. Pin overlap side through all layers to prevent scooting of fabric. Using Scotch tape as a stitching guide, topstitch 1" from CF. When you get to the curve, step on the accelerator and go. It's easier when you stitch fast! Remove tapes.

NOTE: For a perfectly curved topstitiching, use washable marker or chalk to draw around a paper template traced from the pattern tissue stitching line. Tuck template back in pattern envelope to use again.

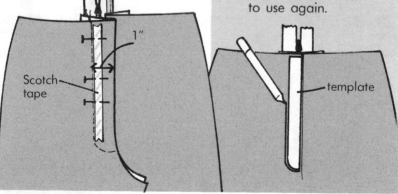

Scotch tape

1"

template

NOTE: We do not feel a "fly protector" is necessary on women's pants unless you use a scratchy metal zipper rather than a smooth synthetic coil zipper. It just adds bulk. For information on a fly protector, see men's fly front section, pg. 120.

The "Never-EVER-Wrinkles" Waistband (our favorite)

Interfacings

Armoflexxx and Ban-Rol are monofilament nylon waistband interfacings available by the yard in ½" to 2" widths. They are lightweight, will not stretch, do not need to be preshrunk, and best of all, they do not roll (even after lunch!) or wrinkle. We buy them by the 50 yard reel!

For stretch fabrics, use Ban-Rol elastic (X-L 90 from Staple Sewing Aids). It is an **elasticized** monofilament nylon waistband interfacing and comes ½"-2" wide also.

> **NOTE:** Pattern companies use 1¼" as their standard waistband width. If you are short waisted or thick in the middle, use a narrower band.

Cut

Don't use your waistband pattern piece. It rarely fits, especially if you bought your pattern by your hip size. Waistband can be cut lengthwise or crosswise with this method, as the interfacing prevents any stretch in the fabric. Cut a rectangle:

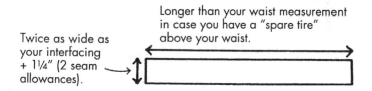

Twice as wide as your interfacing + 1¼" (2 seam allowances).

Longer than your waist measurement in case you have a "spare tire" above your waist.

For example, if you are using 2" interfacing, cut band 5¼" wide.

Sew

1. Mark the ⅝" stitching line on one edge of your band. Machine baste on seamline (fastest) or mark with a washable marker.

waistband

seam line

87

2. Place interfacing next to seam line on wrong side of band. Stitch interfacing to seam allowance. (This step produces the smooth right side appearance.)

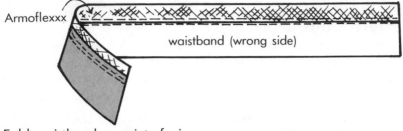

Armoflexxx

waistband (wrong side)

3. Fold waistband over interfacing and fit by wrapping band around your waist and snipping edge of seam allowances where it comes together. This is the center back if your pants have a back opening (or center front for a fly front).

4. Halfway between these snips is the center front (or center back) snip here too.

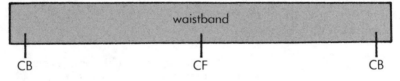

waistband

CB   CF   CB

5. Pin band to pants, matching top edges of band and pant. Place pins horizontally so you can try pants on to check waistband fit.

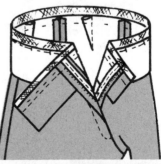

NOTE: Your pants should always be at least one inch larger than band. Easing the pants onto band allows pants to fall more gracefully over hips.

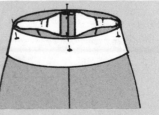

6. Try on. If you have any dimples or wrinkles, unpin band and adjust until they disappear.

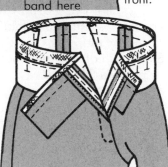

To remove these wrinkles, shift pant toward front.

move pant up into band here

7. Change pins to a vertical position. Stitch on ⅝" seam line as shown with interfacing on top. The feed dogs of your machine will ease pants into band.

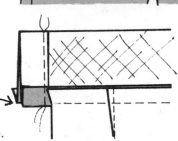

Finish Ends of Band

1. Fold band in half, right sides together. Trim interfacing to stitching line. Stitch next to interfacing. Slip underside of band ⅛" to prevent it from peeking at ends (underside will be smaller so will pull to inside).

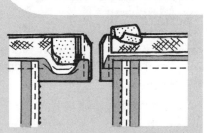

NOTE: The amount of overlap and underlap is up to you. You can sew the overlap side ¹/₁₆" from the center front or back and the underlap 1" from the zipper, or leave a 1" extension on both ends.

¹/₁₆"

1"

NOTE: Before turning waistband right side out, wrap a 2" wide piece of fusible web around the interfacing at ends of waistband. Turn and steam. This will fuse both sides of waistband to interfacing. Now when you sew hooks and eyes in place, they will not pull to the outside and show.

Quick Finish Waistband — "Stitch in the Ditch"

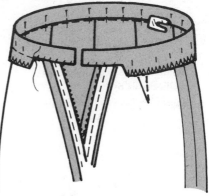

1. Make a ⅝" clip next to ends of waistband. Fold seam allowances under from band end to clip. Pin. Zigzag raw edges of waistband if fabric ravels (or use Fray Check or Seams Great). Pin waistband in place as shown.

2. Topstitch in the well of the seam from right side.

3. Hand slip stitch ends.

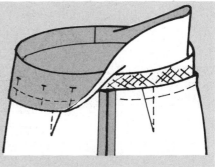

NOTE: The placement of the interfacing keeps the seam allowances from making a ridge on the right side. Now you can see why this method gives you a completely smooth waistband on the outside — even in lightweight fabrics.

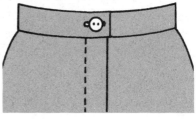

You can sew buttonholes through the monofilament nylon waistband interfacing. Practice on a sample first as the bulk at the end can get in the way. Sew buttons on by machine too.

Stitch Hooks and Eyes on by Machine

They will stay on better and won't show under a belt. Tape in place with Scotch tape and use a narrow zigzag stitch.

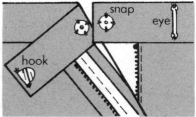

Add a snap to the extension to hold it in place — snaps can be machine zigzagged too!

More Tips

1. Does this happen to you? Before finishing the wrong side of band, close zipper and put a pin where bands should come together. Restitch until even.

2. Do you get this pull at the top? Sew hook or button tighter and instantly solve the problem!

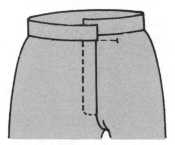 

3. **Belt loops the easy way!** Cut one long strip 1" wide. Press under ¼" on each side and fold in half again. Press. OR, cut with one edge on selvage, fold in thirds. Stitch on both edges.

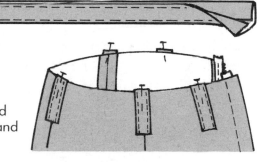

Cut belt loops the desired length.

Pin or baste at side seams, center back and between center front and back.

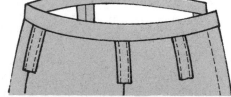

Stitch waistband to pants.

Bring belt carriers to wrong side and hand overcast in place.

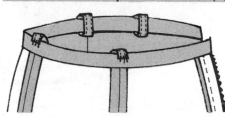

Quick Fusible Waistbands

Waist Shaper® and Fuse 'n Fold® are nonwoven waistband interfacings perforated on stitching and folding lines for easy use. Pati (with her small waist and larger hips) finds these unsatisfactory as they wrinkle on her, but Susan (who is more straight up and down) loves fusible waistband interfacings and never has the wrinkling problem. Try both the monofilament nylon interfacings and the fusibles and see which YOU like best.

Contour Waistbands

Contour bands are shaped sections at the top of pants that are curved to fit your body. Commercial patterns may not be curved the same as you are so fit a contour band before cutting so it will lie smoothly.

Fit by holding the yoke pattern up to your body and tucking in or splitting the pattern until it lies smoothly, or cut band pieces out of Featherweight Pellon and fit.

1. Divide pattern into equal sections.

2. Slash and spread band pattern until it fits you. To make larger, insert tissue and tape in place.

3. Slash and overlap to make smaller. Tape in place.

NOTE: When stitching band to pants, prevent stretch of these curved seams by sewing through seam tape placed over seam lines.

If your pants fit properly, you can turn up the same amount of hem on both legs. If one leg is longer, compensate at the waistline, not at the hemline (pg. 45). Hem depth should be 1½-2" for fashion pants, more will weight your stitches, causing them to show.

4 Rules For an Invisible Hem

1. Trim seam allowance in hem area to ¼" to eliminate bulk.

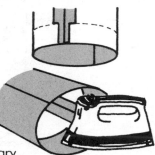

2. Never press over top edge of hem — you'll get a ridge on right side. Press from fold to ½" from hem edge.

3. Finish raw edge **only** if necessary.

4. Use polyester or poly/cotton thread. It wears longer and you'll never have a hem come out because of a broken thread.

Different Hems for Different Uses

1. Use the designer hem stitch (our favorite because it's the most invisible). Take long loose staggered stitches (these stitches are under the hem edge) catching only a single fiber of your outside fabric. You can do this if you use the smallest needle you can thread — a size 10 sharp is best.

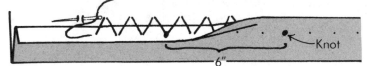

Knot

6"

> **NOTE:** Every 6", pull to loosen stitches so they will be more invisible and secure by knotting in hem allowance. This protects you in case you accidentally step into your hem.

2. Use your machine blind hemmer for a very sturdy hem, best for medium to heavy fabrics. It's great for children's clothes or for pants that will be machine washed and dried frequently.

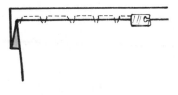

3. Use fusible web for a very fast hem, good for doubleknits, children's things, work clothes. Cut web ¼" narrower than the hem width. Fuse 10-15 seconds in each spot to within ¼" of top edge. Test on a scrap first to make sure fusible web won't be too stiff.

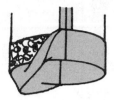

Finishing the Hem Edge
(from least durable to most durable)

Least durable — for fabrics that are hand washed, drycleaned, don't ravel or are lined. This category will be most invisible.

None — for knits

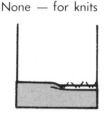

Pink — less is best for light-weight wovens

Stitch and pink for heavy cottons and wools

More durable — for fabrics that ravel and/or are machine washed.

Zigzag — for medium fabrics.

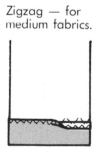

Triple zigzag for lightweight fabrics that a zigzag might bunch up.

Seams Great or Seams saver. See pg. for application.

Most durable — for fabrics that really ravel and will get hard wear. These hem and finish in one step.

Turn under full hem and machine topstitch 1 or 2 rows.

Trim hem allowance to ½". Turn up ¼" twice. Press. Topstitch or top-stitch and edgestitch.

Why Line or Underline

1. To prevent seams and underwear from showing through light colors. Underlining does this best as it also cushions seam allowances.

2. To keep wools from scratching or causing allergies. Lining gives the most complete coverage.

3. To strengthen loosely woven or fragile fabrics. Underlining works best because it is sewn into all seams next to the outer fabric.

4. To prevent baggy knees and seat. Underlining is best for same reason as above.

5. To prevent wrinkling — either will do the job.

Underline with . . .
Poly-SiBonne Plus
Cotton or poly/cotton
   batiste or light-
   weight broadcloth
Polyester lining

For more body . . .
Veriform Durable Press
Armo Press
Keynote Plus

Underlining
1. Baste underlining to wrong side of fashion fabric.

2. Sew pants treating the two layers as one.

Line with . . .
Polyester lining or
blouse weight fabrics:
   Butterfly
   Ciao
   Coupe de Ville
Poly/cotton batiste

Lining
1. Sew pants out of lining. Sew pants out of fashion fabric.

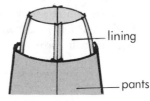

2. Place the two pants wrong sides together and sew them at waist and hem.

Instant Underlining with the Glue and Fold Method

Use Sobo, the fabric glue that dries soft and flexible. Sobo is permanent, so only use on the seam allowances.

1. Cut underlining and fashion fabric from the same pattern piece.

2. Mark darts on underlining only.

3. Steam press the two layers together to remove wrinkles and excess shrinkage caused by steam.

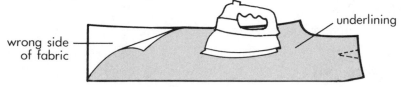

underlining

wrong side of fabric

4. Lift the underlining and dot Sobo glue (open nozzle only ¼ turn for **small** dots) on the seam allowances close to the edge of fabric.

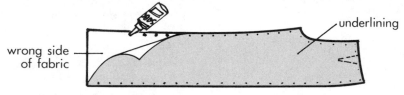

underlining

wrong side of fabric

5. Because the underlining is like an inner cylinder when on the body, it must be made smaller or it will sag. Quickly, before the glue dries, fold each leg lengthwise toward the center front or back. A small bubble will form in the underlining.

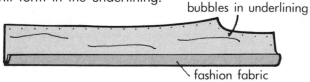

bubbles in underlining

fashion fabric

6. Fold again and the bubble will get larger.

7. Scoot excess underlining (the bubble) off the edge while glue is still wet. Let each leg remain folded until dry (5 min.) Cut off excess underlining if it gets in your way.

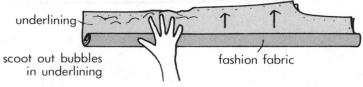

underlining

scoot out bubbles in underlining

fashion fabric

8. After glue dries, baste through center of dart, ½" past dart point in order to catch both layers when stitching dart.

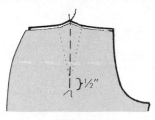

> **NOTE:** The dart may have moved a small amount toward the center. It's not enough to worry about.

9. Sew pants together treating the two layers as one. When you turn up hem, underlining will scoot out a bit as another inner cylinder is created. This is why we didn't have you glue hem edge.

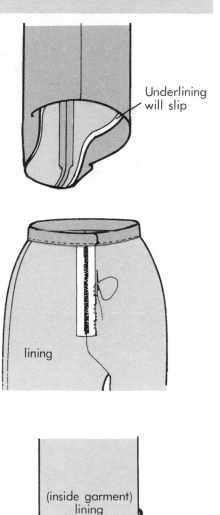

Underlining will slip

Pro Tips for Linings

1. After attaching waistband, hand slip stitch lining to zipper tape.

2. The lining should always be cut the length of finished garment. When turned up it will ALWAYS be shorter than the garment and not show.

lining

3. A "jump hem" is a tidy way to finish lined pant. Hem garment first, then turn under lining to desired length and pin about one inch away from fold. Fold lining back to pins and slip stitch lining to garment hem with a long hemming stitch. Be sure to catch only lining hem allowance and not lining itself.

(inside garment) lining

garment hem

18 Terrific Trousers

Terrific Trousers

Do you realize that trousers are the most flattering pant style we can wear? They are, because the details and the extra fullness in the front camouflage our lumps and bumps.

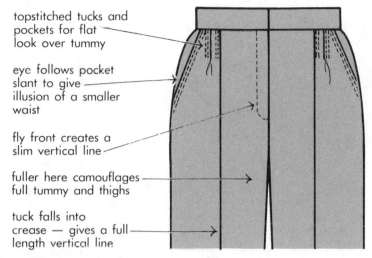

topstitched tucks and pockets for flat look over tummy

eye follows pocket slant to give illusion of a smaller waist

fly front creates a slim vertical line

fuller here camouflages full tummy and thighs

tuck falls into crease — gives a full length vertical line

An Illusion Trick

Trousers will hang straight down from your tummy because of the extra fullness in the front.

The front leg is cut wider at the side and at the front inseam.

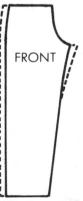

FRONT

This will happen if your trousers are too tight. Add to front inseam for less tummy emphasis.

Anyone can wear trousers and look good in them IF they fit and IF the details are well done. However, because of all the details, we don't recommend that you sew your first pair of pants using a trouser style pattern. First, learn more about your body using a simple basic style. Then, concentrate on sewing flattering trousers.

Snip mark when cutting trousers for speed and accuracy.

This will save you an hour of sewing time. Snip ⅛"-¼" into cut edge at the following places.

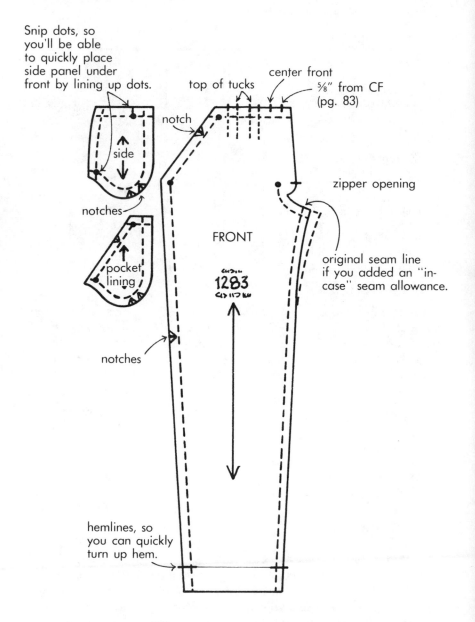

Snip dots, so you'll be able to quickly place side panel under front by lining up dots.

top of tucks

center front
⅝" from CF
(pg. 83)

notch

side

notches

pocket lining

notches

FRONT

1283

zipper opening

original seam line if you added an "in-case" seam allowance.

hemlines, so you can quickly turn up hem.

Tuck Tricks

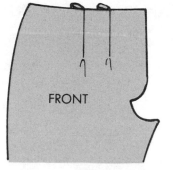

1. A classic trouser pattern has 2 tucks but that doesn't mean you must have 2 tucks. Convert them to 3 smaller tucks, 1 larger tuck, or if you have a thick waist, leave them out entirely for more room around the middle. If narrower tucks look better on you, sew tucks narrower, then take side seams in later during fitting if waist is too big.

FRONT

2. Press tucks toward side (the opposite direction of darts). The fullness is then pushed to the side and not over tummy.

3. Topstitch tucks flat in a "U" shape 1½"-2½" down from the waist. Tucks will now be flat over your tummy.

4. Topstitch top of pocket to side panel the same distance from the waist as tucks. Pocket will now stay flat over tummy.

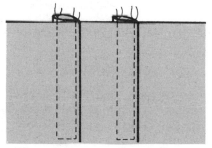

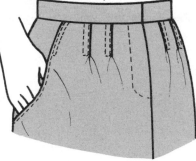

Tidy Trouser Pockets

Trim and turn pocket. Slip an extra ¹/₁₆" to inside so lining won't show.

Topstitch edge to hold lining inside pocket.

Pin side panel under front, lining up snips. Lower edges probably will not match. Let them fall where they want to. Pin flat and stitch.

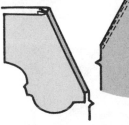

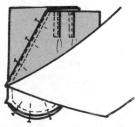

Prevent Pocket Gaposis

There are two reasons why trouser pockets gap:

1. They don't fit your shape. Pattern companies test fit on a perfect size 10 fitting model who is probably curved differently than you.

   Cut out and pin pieces together. **Very** carefully try on pants.

If pockets gap	Pin tucks deeper to	**OR**	Move front panel down on side panel. (This won't noticeably affect grain.)

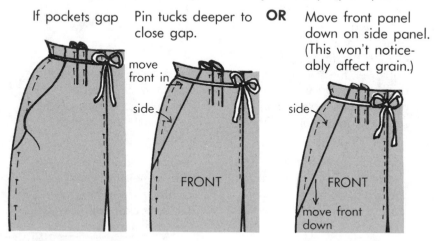

2. The pocket edge is on the bias and will stretch when you put your hands in your pockets.

   To prevent stretch, tape pocket edge with seam tape.

Pin pocket lining to front. Pin one end of tape. Mark a dot on lining and another on tape ⅛"-¼" apart.	Pull tape until marks line up. Pin, distributing fullness. Sew with tape on top, machine will ease edge to tape.

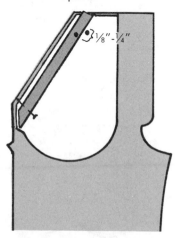
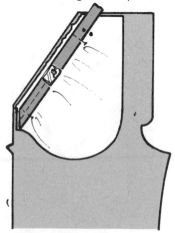

Add a Trouser Stay

Turn your pocket into a front stay! The stay will be caught in the zipper, keeping the tucks and pocket flat. It will also prevent you from sewing the pants too tight, causing the pleats to pooch.

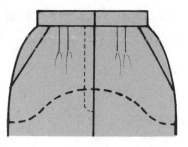

1. Place pocket pattern piece over front pattern piece.

2. Pin tucks out of front.

3. Add tissue to extend pocket pattern piece to center front as shown. Use new stay pattern to cut pocket out of lining.

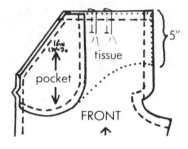

4. After sewing and topstitching tucks and sewing lining to pocket edge, turn stay to wrong side and machine baste to pants at center front (CF).

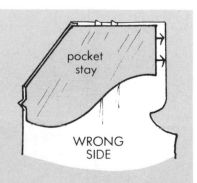

NOTE: If you sew narrower tucks, you will need to add to center front of stay. If you anticipate narrower tucks, add a little extra to center front of stay when cutting "in-case" you need it. Otherwise you'll need to cut a new wider stay.

Use the slide method to add width to a trouser pant.

Pin pattern to fabric. Chalk mark amount needed.

Cut all but side.

Slide pattern to chalk marks and finish cutting sides.

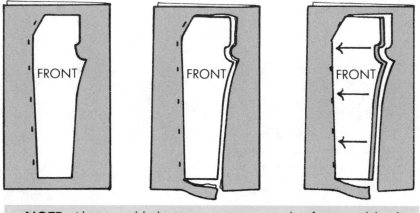

NOTE: Always add the same amount to the front and back. See pg. 20.

The result is the same as slashing the pattern down the middle and spreading it the amount needed, but sliding is faster. Do not add to side panel.

Slide the pattern back to original position to mark tucks or darts. The crease should be halfway between your inseam and outseam and most flattering if it meets one of the tucks.

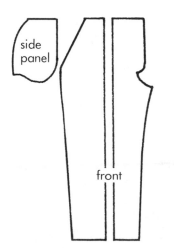

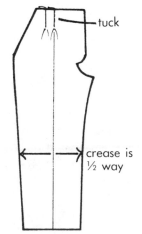

Jumpsuits

Fitting a jumpsuit is the same as fitting a bodice and pants, except the two are joined at the waist.

Pattern Size

Buy a jumpsuit pattern to fit your bustline. It is much easier to alter the pant portion than it is to alter the bodice.

Jumpsuit Styles

If you've never sewn a jumpsuit before, choose a pattern with a waistline seam. Cut a 1" seam allowance onto the waist of the bodice and the pant pieces.

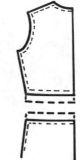

With the larger waistline seam allowances, you can easily alter for all the following:

1. **Sway back** — sew a deeper waistline seam at center back tapering to normal seamline at sides.

2. **Full tummy** — let out waistline at center front tapering to normal seamline at sides.

3. **Jumpsuit too long in crotch** — sew deeper waist seam all way around.

4. **Jumpsuit too short in crotch** — sew shallower waist seam all way around.

> **NOTE:** Raise your arms for the true comfort test of jumpsuit body length. One with sleeves needs more length than one without sleeves.

Fit Bodice Length

1. Pin tissue pattern together — shoulder seams, side seams down to waist, and darts.

2. Tie ¼" elastic around waist. Try on tissue pattern over elastic. Check to see if pattern waist markings come down to bottom of elastic.

3. If waist markings do not meet bottom edge of elastic, lengthen or shorten front and back the necessary amount as shown. This also gives you an opportunity to check dart position and depth of a "V" neckline etc.

front

slash & spread
to lengthen

tuck to
shorten

waist

Fit Width

1. Measure the width of waist and hips of tissue pattern and compare to your own body measurements. Make sure you have at least 2" hip ease if using a woven fabric.

2. Adjust side seams by adding as shown. If you need to make width smaller, take side seams in deeper when sewing.

3. If you only need more waist room, sew narrower darts or eliminate them entirely.

NOTE: Cut 1" side seam allowances (rather than ⅝" if you are not sure how much ease you need.)

Fit Crotch

1. Use your altered basic pant pattern (pg. 50) as a guide. (Now, aren't you glad you spent the time to make a basic!) Lay jumpsuit pattern over pant pattern and line up the crotch lines. Make sure jumpsuit is ¼" longer from crotch to waist than pants.

2. Lengthen or shorten crotch depth if necessary the same way you would a pant (pg. 29).

3. Recommended crotch depth ease for jumpsuit fabrics.

Woven fabrics . . . . ¾" ease
Moderate stretch knits . . . . . ½" ease
Very stretchy knits . . . . ¼" ease

(If they are SUPER stretchy knits like velours you may be better off with no ease.)

NOTE: The chart applies to jumpsuits with sleeves. Sleeveless jumpsuits would have the same amount of crotch depth as pants.

NOTE: It is worse to make a jumpsuit too long in the crotch than too short. If too long wear a belt which would shorten it a little, or take a horizontal tuck at the waist and cover it with a belt. If it is too short, just 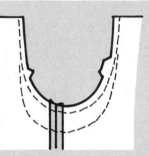 sew a deeper crotch seam as shown. Sew crotch seam deeper ¼" at a time, trim and try on until comfortable. You can lower the crotch up to 2" in a straight leg jumpsuit without effecting width of legs. However, the legs will get shorter, so check hem allowance!

Culottes

Culottes are cut fuller than pants, more like a skirt. Pattern companies automatically make the crotch of culottes ½"-¾" longer than a basic style pant. Make the same alterations on culotte pattern that you made on basic pant pattern. Overlay crotch lines to make sure the crotch of the culotte is longer. The hip width may be wider also, because the culotte is fuller. Remember, you can always make it smaller using fit-as-you-sew!

Differences between a culotte and a pant pattern

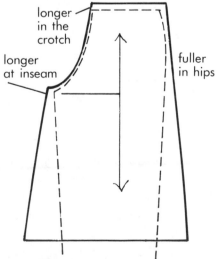

longer in the crotch

longer at inseam

fuller in hips

Three reasons to learn to sew them:

1. **Fit** — Sew them to fit **your** shape! If the waist is always too big, and the crotch too tight, you are a sew-them-yourself jeans body. (pg. 8 for more jeans fit information.)

2. **Price** — Now that jeans (even kids') cost as much as the weekly grocery bill, it will behoove us to learn to copy these easy-to-sew once-you-learn, money savers.

3. **Creativity** — Another reason to sew your own jeans. Go beyond denim, try velveteen, satin, synthetic suedes, or stretch denim. Embroider on the pocket — why wear some designer's name!

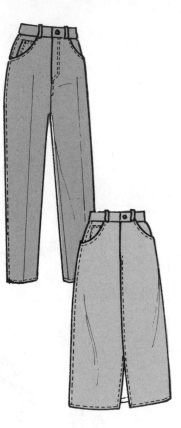

Don't Let All the Pocket Pieces Scare You

Follow this simple order:

Sew pocket to side piece, then side piece to one lining piece.

Sew pocket lining to front

Turn and press. Topstitch.

Place side section under front and stitch side section to pocket lining.

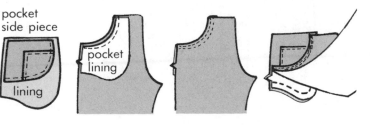

pocket side piece

lining

pocket lining

Special "Fit-As-You-Sew"™ Order for Jeans

We designed a jeans pattern that allows you to fit jeans even with flat felled side seams. We also added "in-case" seam allowances at the upper inseam (for full thighs), side seams (for hip width), and waist (for crotch depth) because jeans are made with less ease in these areas. You can make these changes on any jeans pattern. After all pocket and zipper construction is done on flat pieces, assemble as shown.

Stitch crotch seams. Machine baste inseam. (Note larger seam allowance.)

Pin side seams right sides out, and pin band onto pants. Try on and fit.

Mark sides and waist (pg. 46). Unpin. Remove inseam basting. Flat fell crotch seams.

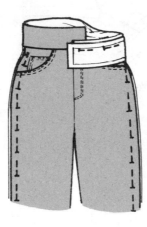

Stitch side seams with mock flat fell seam.

Stitch inseams. Trim to ⅝". Zigzag seam allowances together. Press toward back. Now apply waistband.

Mock flat felled seam: (faster and less bulky)

Sew seam. Trim one side to ¼". Zigzag other edge.

Press to one side, long seam over short. Topstitch close to seam and ¼" away.

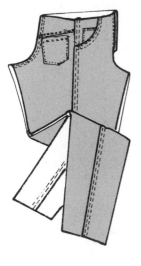

zigzag

Since we are both selfish seamsters treasuring our precious sewing time, when we sew for men it can only be termed "a labor of love!" We try to use fast and easy, yet still professional looking, sewing techniques.

We avoid the traditional fly front, the tailored waistband, and patterns with welt pockets in favor of more streamlined methods.

Our secret — we use the same techniques used in our own pants.

1. The Never Roll waistband technique (pg. 87).

2. The same simple fly front zipper technique as that used in women's pants, just a mirror image (pg. 118).

3. Patch pockets on pant back rather than welt pockets.

Once you master **fitting** men's pants, then you can elaborate more on the **sewing** techniqes.

Pattern Size

Buy a pant pattern by hip size for a better pant leg shape. Add to the waist if necessary. If the pattern includes a jacket, buy by the chest size. It's easier to alter pants than a jacket.

Fitting Pants for Men

Measure waist, hip, and length from waist to floor at sides, and crotch to floor at inseam. You may find it easier to measure a pair of ready-made pants that fit reasonably well. Measure the pant waist, hip, inseam, and outseam. Subtract the inseam from the outseam for crotch depth measurement.

The gingham shell fit concept works for men as well as women! See chapter 5 for women's shell details and read on for the fit differences.

Common Alterations

There are two very common fitting problems in pants for men over 40 years of age. One is the "flat derriere" and the other is the full tummy commonly called the "bay window."

"Bay Window"   **"Flat Derriere"**

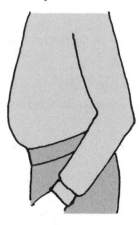 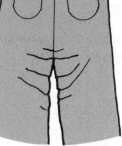

Patterns altered for men commonly look like this:

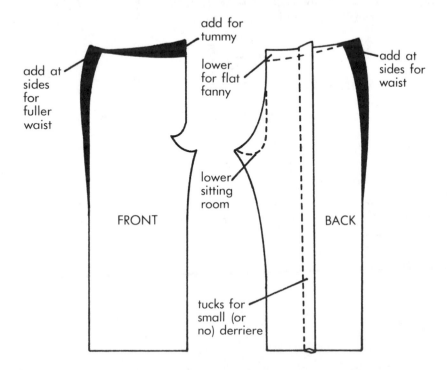

add at sides for fuller waist

add for tummy

lower for flat fanny

lower sitting room

FRONT

add at sides for waist

lower sitting room

BACK

tucks for small (or no) derriere

Sewing Order for Men's Pants

1. Sew fly front first (see pg. 118).

2. Sew inner leg seams together. Press open.

3. Finish sewing crotch seam, but leave a 3" opening at top center back.

4. Pin baste outside seams.

5. Try on for a fitting. Tie ¼" elastic around waistline to hold pants up.

6. Permanently sew all seams. Press open.

7. A man's waistband is usually in two pieces — it's divided at the center back. Apply waistband using the Never Roll method. Use 1½" or 2" wide Armoflexxx or Ban Rol waistband interfacing.

8. Finish sewing back crotch seam through waistband. Press seam open and tack down. This method allows for easy altering later.

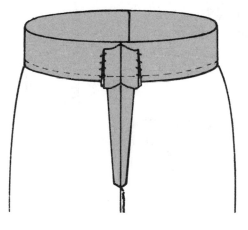

NOTE: Men's patterns usually appear very complicated because of all the pocket pieces (often including a front "watch pocket"). The easiest way to figure out how they are assembled is to **pin the tissue pattern pieces together** before you cut and sew. This helps organize all those little pieces and understand where they go.

Men's Fly Front Zipper

1. A fly front zipper is like a lapped zipper. A woman's fly laps right over left (pg. 83) and a man's fly laps left over right. Also, a fly protector is added as the last step.

   There is an overlap and an underlap. The fold line on the overlap side is the center front (CF).

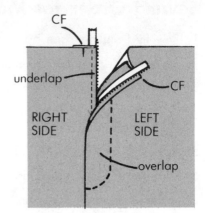

2. Check your pattern before cutting. The fly front extension should measure at least 1½" wide so it will be caught in topstitching. If fly front is not 1½" wide, add width when cutting.

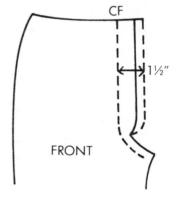

3. Snip mark fold lines: Snip CF for overlap, snip ⅝" from CF for underlap. (This fold is even with crotch line cut edge.)

4. Use a 12" conventional zipper. Let the excess extend above the top edge and into waistband and cut off later. With deep underlap, zipper won't show so a perfect color match isn't necessary.

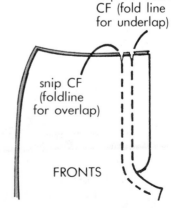

Front Fly Zipper For Men

1. Stitch crotch seam 1½" from inseam to zipper opening. Backstitch.

2. Fold left front under from crotch seam to center front (CF) snip. Press. Fold right front under from underlap snip to edge of crotch seam allowance.

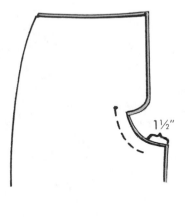

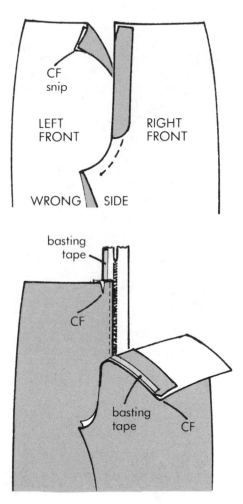

3. Place basting tape on underlap side of zipper. Peel away protective paper and stick to underlap. Stitch next to fold.

4. Place basting tape on edge of overlap. Peel away protective paper.

5. Line up CF snips and stick overlap in place.

6. Flip overlap out of way and pin zipper to extension only. Stitch from zipper side (this is reinforcement stitching).

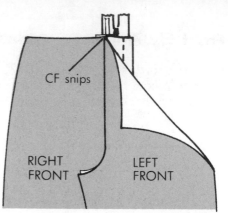

RIGHT FRONT

LEFT FRONT

CF snips

7. Lay fronts on flat surface. Pin overlap side through all layers to prevent scooting of fabric. Using Scotch® Brand Magic Transparent® Tape as a stitching guide. Topstitch 1" from CF. When you get to the curve, step on the accelerator and go. It's easier when you stitch fast. Remove tapes.

NOTE: For a perfectly curved topstitching, use washable marker or chalk to draw around a paper template traced from the pattern tissue stitching line. Tuck template back in pattern envelope to use again.

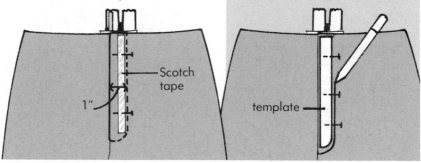

Scotch tape

1"

template

8. Insurance for men! Cut fly protector according to pattern and sew lining fabric to rounded edge. Turn and press. Sew fly protector to extension on underlap side.

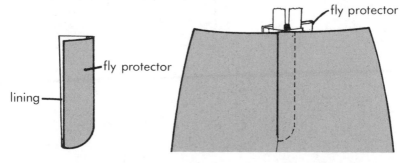

fly protector

fly protector

lining

If you have a pattern that you've altered to fit and then your weight changes, can you still sew from the same pattern? Can you adjust the pants you've already made? Yes and yes! You can adjust most pants within the seam allowances for up to 10 pounds weight change and your basic and other patterns for up to 20 pounds weight change.

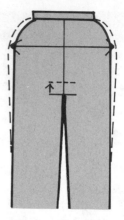

What Happens When You Gain or Lose Weight

If you gain weight, your body expands. As you fill out the pants the crotch gets shorter. If you lose weight, you deflate in width and the crotch will hang lower.

1. Take waistband off and side seams out. Pin sides to fit, raise or lower elastic until waistband is comfortable. Mark new side and waist seams.

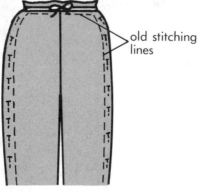

old stitching lines

2. If you've lost weight, you can easily sew waistband down lower to shorten crotch, but if you've gained weight, you may not have enough seam allowance to sew waistband higher. Sew crotch lower instead ¼" at a time, trim seam allowance to ¼", and try on until it is comfortable.

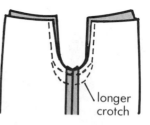

longer crotch

Now make the same changes on the pattern you used to make the pants.

Change Your Basic Pattern

It's easy! Just try on your gingham pant, refit it, and mark new seam lines on your basic pattern.

You Don't Have a Basic Pattern

You have many favorite patterns you've sewed over and over. If you have gained weight, cut 1" seam allowances on the top and at the sides in order to have room to adjust if needed. If you have lost weight, cut the pattern out as you always have and sew deeper side seams and waistband on lower during fit-as-you-sew.

Style Changes Also Change Fit

About every 7 years pant styling shifts from "derriere fit" toward the "trouser style," and pattern companies redraft their master patterns or slopers to accommodate the new look. For example, the shaded area is the fitted pant in this illustration. This fashion shift can change your alterations and you may need to make a new basic shell. Pati found that in the early 70's she barely had to add anything for her "thighus gigantus" due to the very full legs on pants. So the alterations you make today are subject to change tomorrow!!

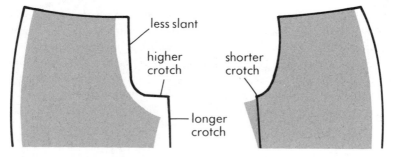

less slant

higher crotch

shorter crotch

longer crotch

Can We Change Our Shape?

Yes! We can change in weight. One of our favorite sayings is "A moment on the lips, a lifetime on the hips." We can also exercise and smooth out the figure. One of Pati's favorite pant exercises is to do side leg lifts while she is brushing her teeth, washing dishes, or fusing interfacings.

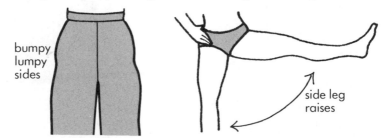

bumpy lumpy sides

side leg raises

But, the easiest way of all to change our shape is to create the illusion of svelt by wearing pants that fit!

Gail Brown, resident maternity expert and author, gives these pant suggestions for mothers-to-be.

Since pregnancy is many different sizes, adjustable pants are a must. Pull-on pants with elastic tied at the side seam can grow with you.

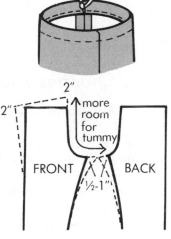

Sew pull-on pants (pg. 52). To convert a basic pant into a maternity pant, add the amounts shown when cutting (This is very similar to a large tummy alteration, (pg. 34).

2"

2" more room for tummy

FRONT BACK

½-1"

Stretch panels are best for when you are biggest, or for converting conventional pants into maternity pants. Some patterns allow for a stretch panel but the panel may not be where you are the largest. Hold the pant front pattern piece up to you and mark around your tummy. Stitch the panel to that marking. Remember, the lower the panel, the longer your tops must be to cover it.

To convert conventional pants to maternity pants, try on pants, chalk mark around your tummy, cut away. Sew a stretch panel in the hole! Great for making maternity jeans, since the ready-made ones are so expensive.

chalk marks

If the stretch panel is too large in the early stages of pregnancy, take tucks at the top or tighten the elastic.

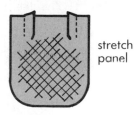

stretch panel

"Be gorgeous," says Gail, who sewed a wool gabardine pant with a stretch panel front! "I got so tired of the stretch pajama look, that I craved crisp fabrics for a change. They made me feel terrific!"

You can alter ready-made clothes, but some alterations are just not worth the time they take — you would be better off sewing from scratch with all the ripping and re-stitching. Here are some adjustments you might consider in order of ease, number one being the easiest.

1. Length — this is the easiest. See page 94 for invisible hems.

2. Width — if the pants are just a little tight and yet they don't have much seam allowance, buy the next size larger and take in the side seams. You may need to remove the waistband first. Too loose to begin with? Just take in side seams.

3. Hips too large, but fit in waist — sew deeper side seams through hip area. If your waist is larger, it may be easier to buy to fit waist and take hips in. If you buy to fit hips, there may not be enough room in the waist or waistband to let out to fit you.

4. Crotch too short — sew crotch deeper (pg. 110). Check hem allowance first as legs may end up shorter.

5. Crotch too long — remove waistband and sew it lower all the way around. This will definitely shorten legs. Check hem allowance.

6. Waist large, but fit in the hips — remove waistband and sew side seams deeper at waist. Sew band back onto pant.

7. Smiles in the crotch — let out inseams as much as possible. Extreme smiles? Definitely don't buy them or toss if you own them!

8. Baggy in the back — remove waistband from side seam to side seam and sew back lower. Still baggy? Take in inseams. Susan's quickie method — just take a tuck right at waistband edge at center back tapering to nothing at side seams. Press toward band.

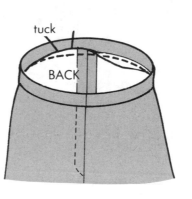

9. Altering lined pants — double the time it takes for any other alteration.

Because skirts fit the same part of your body, you will make the same adjustments on skirts as you would on pants.

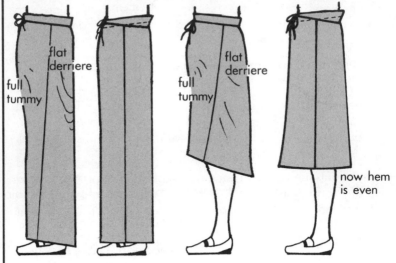

flat derriere

full tummy

flat derriere

full tummy

now hem is even

Pull down in front and up in back until wrinkles are gone and side seams are straight. You'll find the same amount of adjustment is needed on both skirts and pants.

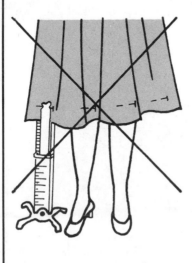

Another lesson we learned about skirts after studying pant fit is that you can **throw away your skirt marker**. Hems are evened at the top not at the bottom (unless they are bias). Making the skirt even at the bottom would not eliminate the wrinkles and the crooked side seam. So once you learn about your body, you can just turn up the same amount of hem all the way around in confidence. Your skirt will automatically be even!

Index